Abjection and Abandonment

Melancholy in Philosophy and Art

Abjection and Abandonment

Melancholy in Philosophy and Art

Edited By

Saitya Brata Das

AAKAR

Abandonment and Abjection: Melancholy in Philosophy and Art
Edited by Saitya Brata Das

First Published 2018

ISBN 978-93-5002-538-3

The publication of this book financially benefits from the University Grants Commission under the Special Assistance Program (SAP) that is granted to the Centre for English Studies, Jawaharlal Nehru University.

Published by
AAKAR BOOKS
28 E Pocket IV, Mayur Vihar Phase I
Delhi 110 091, India
aakarbooks@gmail.com
www.aakarbooks.com

Designed by
Limited Colors, Delhi 110 092

Printed at
D.K. Fine Art Press, Delhi 110 052

Contents

Editor's Introduction

Saitya Brata Das

For long, since the inception of "philosophy", the question of melancholy is intimately connected with creativity. Thus, Aristotle could say that creative people—poets and philosophers—are melancholic people. The great Renaissance thinker, the Platonist par excellence, Marsilio Ficcino re-interprets this idea in his own terms and in his own manner: one who is born under Saturn tends to be melancholic, and such an individual also tends to be philosophical. There is a certain austerity and severity, and something hermetic about this mysterious planet Saturn which is considered to be the farthest planet in the solar system in those days: like the slow movement of Saturn and its irreducible distance, the philosopher is slow and distant, looking at the farthest horizon of being. But this affirmative or positive idea of melancholy is not the only one in its history: it passes through the medieval conception of *acedia* which is not cosmologically interpreted but interpreted as part of spiritual health or lack of it. Similarly following Ficcino, we have Shakespeare's great contemporary Ben Jonson who in his hilarious *Everyman in His Humour* makes fun of the fashionable postures that erudite and learned individuals of his time display: here the traditional theory of four humours which was about the physical constitution of the human—and we know a great deal about this from Galen and Robert Burton—is here theatricalised and made humorous, humour that is cultivated to the extreme point of hilarity. And this is remarkable since the play was written around the same time as Hamlet. Hamlet who, as we know, is the melancholic individual par excellence who, not surprisingly, is also the philosopher. His melancholy makes him unable to set things right, things that are out of joint, as if there is something worklessness about melancholy. That is why despite Freud's great departure from the traditional conceptions of melancholy—melancholy as the lack of spiritual health, melancholy as the astrological-cosmological connection, melancholy as theatricalised postures of learned individuals—Freud still retains the conception of work, though he transforms it in his own manner. In his distinction of mourning from melancholy where mourning is famously understood in relation to the possibility of work—*Trauerarbeit* –melancholy remains workless, and hence needs therapy. This point in the history of the question of melancholy marks a radical change. The dominant schools of Psychoanalysis have carried this even further: melancholy becomes identical to what has come to be called "depression" and later even "clinical depression" in psychiatry. I can't draw out here all the consequences of this here.

In the early twentieth century both Martin Heidegger and Walter Benjamin, each in his own manner and independently, have brought out the consequences out of the Freudian discourse. In the Heideggerian 'analytic' of truth as disclosure—and no longer as *adaequatio* of the predicative proposition—which demands deconstruction of the metaphysics of the subject, the fundamental attunement—*Grundstimmung*—of melancholy is understood as the very opening that attunes us to being. My German speaking friends will be sympathetic to me, so I hope, for translating *Stimmung* as attunement and not as 'mood': the musical metaphor here is indispensable for both Heidegger and Benjamin, albeit in different ways. While Benjamin draws this musical metaphor from Leibniz—that is, Benjamin's unique Leibniz, Heideggerian *Stimmung* is drawn from the Hölderlinian *Grundstimmung* of mourning: the divine mourning at the wake of the flight of Gods. Here in the Heideggerian interpretation of Hölderlinian *Grundstimmung* mourning is no longer understood to belong to the metaphysics of the subject, but as the event of being in its withdrawal from presence. Heidegger deepens this idea of *Stimmung* in his later writings, especially in his reflections on language. Taking up the Meister Eckhart's thought of *Gelassenheit* Heidegger translates it into the idea of abandonment: there is a melancholy in letting-being-be, that is, in releasement or renouncing the appropriation of being by man. The poetizing language of the poets and the thinking-language of the thinkers are, thus, in a profound manner, melancholic: this melancholy, as the opening to the arrival of being, is before any distinction between sadness and happiness, pessimism and optimism. The naming language of poetizing and the naming language of thinking, in their two-fold manner and in the neighbourhood, withdraw and give up—the *lassen* of *Gelassenheit*—the metaphysical violence of the concept.

Similarly and yet differently, Benjamin too thinks naming—the Adamic naming—as the pure event of language as the language of truth. Truth is as much irreducible to knowledge as ideas are irreducible to concepts: the naming language of truth keeps alive—like a secret password that passes from God to the human and to nature, like a secret password that passes from generation to generation through proper naming—the promise of redemption. There is a melancholy—a paradisiacal melancholy—that adheres to the language of naming; there is, however, another melancholy, that erupts as the consequence of the Fall: naming turns out to be overnaming and becomes judgment, and the paradisiacal melancholy of naming becoming the overwhelming melancholy of history and nature that suffer that violence of judgment. It is in the naming language of poetry and of philosophy, and in works of translation which translates not the-what of language but the way of language, that there remains the remnants of the truth which, in remembrance, is restituted and fulfilled. Benjamin names this messianic fulfilment "redemption".

Thus, the question of melancholy is inextricably connected with a host of other questions: melancholy and language, melancholy and violence, and thus, law and judgment, melancholy and the most fascinating theological-messianic conception of redemption as the critique of historical Reason, the melancholy of things, and above all, the melancholy in relation to the questions of work and death. Schelling, even before Heidegger, in his great book on freedom, thinks of the irreducible veil of melancholy, not only of man and nature, but the melancholy—though the possibility of it and not its actuality—of God himself. Melancholy marks, as it were, the very nexus of beings, or the breaking of this nexus. Schelling here in a profound manner is influenced by the German mystic Jacob Böhme: the abyss—*abgrund*—that lies in Godhead itself! The melancholy of the mortal lies in her not being able to completely actualize the possibilities, but the mortal in her freedom that turns demonic, attempt to exhaust all the possibilities into being, so that no non-being may remain un-actualized. But herein precisely lies the radical evil. In that sense, the irreducible melancholy of the mortal that constantly reminds him that his mortality shelters him from the malicious hunger of evil where the abyss of human freedom turns demonic.

To think again of this fascinating question of melancholy in the light of contemporary thought was the task of the one day conference held on 3 March, 2017. This edited volume has grown out of the contributions at the conference, and some of the contributions here are especially invited papers for the volume. Almost all the contributions are trans-disciplinary in nature, drawing on different disciplines like Psychoanalysis, Cultural Theory, Medical Studies, Sociological Studies and Aesthetic Theories. The trans-disciplinary nature of this volume, it is hoped, will make it an interesting and fruitful experience for the readers.

Melancholy Philosophy
Polis-Praxis-Phronesis and the Slave's Know-How

Anup Dhar

This paper places "philosophy" at the cusp of the "act of mourning" and the "fact of melancholia". The paper argues that one side of philosophy has, as if, completed the act of mourning for what it (has) lost. *What* has it lost is, however, the question: has it lost, as Arendt (2005) in *The Promise of Politics* suggests, the old and short-lived Socratic urge to *be in the polis*, be in polis life; to lead a life tied to the polis, tied to life in the polis? Has it lost its touch with, as Marx (2002 [1845]) in *Theses on Feuerbach* suggests, *praxis*; or as Tagore (2011 [1925]) in Prospectus for 'A Viswa-Bharati Institute for Rural Reconstruction at Sriniketan' suggests, *coordination of brain and hand*? Has it lost touch with, as Heidegger (1985) in *Being and Time* suggests, *phronesis*? Has it lost its contact, as Lacan (2007) in *The Other Side of Psychoanalysis* suggests, with the "slave", with slave life-worlds, and especially with the slave's "know-how"? This side of philosophy has, as if, moved on, with manic[1] determination to the side of *theoria*, *sophia*, or *episteme*. It has in turn led to the hyper-separation of "thought and action" (Arendt 2005) and the world of knowing (*theoria*), world of making (*poiesis*) and the world of doing (*praxis*) (Carr 2006). 'The Other Side of Philosophy'[2] has, as if, remained melancholic about what it (has) lost. One side of philosophy, the official side triumphs over the loss through mourning.

The Other side of philosophy remains haunted by the loss/lost. The image (*imago*) of the lost, or the shadow of the loss works as a haunting rem(a)inder over this side of philosophy and there is melancholia; this side of philosophy finds itself identified with an object of a *jouissance* from which it cannot separate itself (Lacan 1990). What, however, is to remain melancholic?

This paper takes off from Freud's 1917 piece 'Mourning and Melancholia' (*Trauer und Melancholie*)[3] to explore the structural distinction between "mourning" and "melancholia". One note of caution: the psychoanalytic perspective and the psychoanalytic experience put to question the standard way of clubbing (/reducing) and confusing all or most states of sadness, withdrawn-ness, inhibition, passivity, quietness, solitudinal proclivity into a catch-all represent-all psychiatric category called "depression". It is not that psychoanalysts do not deploy the concept of depression in their work. That, however, would be psychiatrized psychoanalysis. Psychoanalysis could be practiced in a psychiatrized or a psychologized form. Most often than not that is the case. Freudian psychoanalysis (*not* psychiatrized or psychologized psychoanalysis), however, with its infinite attention to the workings of the unconscious would mark the differences in the analysand's experience and condition much more carefully, in more detail and with depth. One such fine distinction is that between mourning and melancholia. This attention to, on the one hand, the fine structural distinction in psychoanalysis and, on the other, of psychoanalysis' resistance to the category depression has of late assumed an "ethical urgency", partly in view of the globalizing of the "non-differentiating cloak of depression" and the mass consumerism of so-called "happiness pills" (Skriabine 1997; Miller 2007). Skriabine (1997) sees depression as 'no more than one of the symptoms of the discontent[s] in civilization' resulting from its 'invasion by the discourse of science and from the precariousness, stressed by Lacan, of our mode of *jouissance*' (Lacan 1990). Depression, like fever, is a *symptom*; it is a symptom of something deeper, something hidden.

Freud searches for the hidden or deeper causality. He reaches, through an archaeology of our experience of and response to loss, the structural distinction between mourning and melancholia. He shows how to the same experience, loss (loss of a loved person, loss of some abstraction such as one's country, liberty, an ideal, etc.), there could be two responses[4]; one where the loss gets sublimated and the ego (re)covers (from) the loss, the lost is replaced by a *new* "found". Freud calls this "act" mourning. The other is where the shadow of the loss (not just the shadow of the lost object: this is why Freud says that the deeper question in the anatomy of loss is not *who* is lost but *what* is lost) prevails, *longue durée* (because the existence of the lost object [or of loss] is psychically prolonged), like a self-consuming self-cannibalizing shadow over the everyday workings of the ego. Freud calls this the blocked dialectic of melancholia. What, however, is the structural distinction between mourning and melancholia? 'The distinguishing mental features of melancholia are a profoundly painful dejection, cessation of interest in the outside world, loss of the capacity to love, inhibition of all activity, and a lowering of the self-regarding feelings to a degree that finds utterance in self-reproaches and self-revilings, and culminates in a delusional expectation of punishment. This picture becomes more intelligible when we consider that, with one exception, the same traits are met with in mourning. *The disturbance of self-regard is absent in mourning*; but otherwise the features are the same' (Freud 1953: 153; italics mine).

> The melancholic displays something else besides which is lacking in mourning—an extraordinary diminution in his self-regard, an impoverishment of his ego on a grand scale. In mourning it is the world which has become poor and empty; in melancholia it is the ego itself. The patient represents his ego to us as worthless, incapable of any achievement and morally despicable; he reproaches himself, vilifies himself and expects to be cast out and punished. He abases himself before everyone and commiserates with his own relatives for being connected with anyone so unworthy. He is not of the opinion that a change has taken place in him, but extends his self-criticism back over the past; he declares that he was never any better. … *one part of the ego sets itself over against the other*, judges it critically, and, as it were, takes it as its object. (Freud 1953: 153; italics mine)

The 'economics of pain' or of suffering is thus different in mourning and in melancholia.[5] Mourning is driven by the teleological: 'when the work of mourning is completed the ego becomes free and uninhibited again'. In melancholia, however, the dialectic is, as if blocked, halted, prolonged in an interminable way: the ego is never freed from the 'delusion of (mainly moral) inferiority' ('there is [however] no correspondence ... between the degree of self-abasement and its real justification'). Mourning is conscious; melancholia is unconscious: 'melancholia is in some way related to an object-loss which is withdrawn from consciousness, in contradistinction to mourning, in which there is nothing about the loss that is unconscious'. Freud shows, how in melancholia, 'the free libido was not displaced on to another object; it was withdrawn *into* the ego. There ... it served to establish an *identification* of the ego with the abandoned object. Thus the shadow of the object fell upon the ego, and the latter could henceforth be judged by a special agency, as though it were an *object*, the forsaken object. In this way an *object-loss*[6] was transformed into an *ego-loss* and the conflict between the ego and the loved person into a cleavage between the critical activity of the ego and the ego as altered by identification' (Freud 1953: 159). The conflict between the ego and the lost object has, as if, been translated, displaced in melancholia into a conflict between one part of the ego with another part of the ego (blame had become self-blame; the lack in the Other had become lack-in-self: "Why did he go away? Did I not love him enough?" "Was I not good enough?", "Where did I lack" emerge as questions). It had become a conflict *within:* between ego and alter ego, between two mirror ego-s, one representing the object and the other the subject, the object register cannibalizing the subject register. The lost Other is not lost, the loss is circumvented; the Other is, as if, lodged *within* the ego, or *as* ego, as a *part* of the ego through identification: 'people never willingly abandon a libidinal position'. Even if the object is lost, the object-libido is retained: it is either *introjected* a la Klein or *incorporated* a la Abraham-Torok into the ego[7]. Crypted in the ego is the tombstone of the lost or of loss, though walled up, buried, buried alive. It is, as if, a topographical arrangement that has been made to keep (conserve-hide) the *living dead*; it is, as if, a sepulcher had been erected, a commemorative monument as rem(a)inder of the Other, but which, paradoxically, marked the spot of an extreme *jouissance,* a sinister *jouissance*, a pleasure entirely *real* : "real" in the Lacanian sense (in the sense of being *inassimilable*, in the sense of being reminiscent of a *void*). The ego is, thus, a repository of *ghost effects*, of an interminable experience of the *hauntological*.

The introjected or incorporated Other, the shadow of the Other on the ego is in conflict with the self. There is, as Girindrasekhar Bose (1948, 1951, 1952) suggests, an internal compass marked by the *see-saw* of the double ego, the doubled up ego, and the irreducible *dwaita-ta* ("two-ness", like the Irigarayan "two lips", and not *dwitva*, or binarisms) of an interiority of ambivalence or an ambivalent interiority: love hate, Other-love self-hate, sadism masochism forming what Bose calls the ambivalence of the *double wish*. 'If the love for the object—a love which cannot be given up though the object itself is given up—takes refuge in narcissistic identification, then the hate comes into operation on this substitutive object, abusing it, debasing it, making it suffer and deriving sadistic satisfaction from its suffering. The self-tormenting in melancholia, which is without doubt enjoyable, signifies ... a satisfaction of trends of sadism and hate which relate to an object, and which have been turned round upon the subject's own self' (Freud 1953: 161-162). The paper argues that one side of philosophy—one could call it *The Other Side of Philosophy*—suffers from this constitutive ambivalence (Bose 1949), so symptomatic of melancholia. The three preconditions of melancholia: the loss of the object a la Freud/loss of love for the object a la Žižek, ambivalence and the regression of the libido into the ego, i.e. the turning of object-loss into ego-loss could help us look into philosophy, its conflicted history and its ambivalent proclivities—with respect to its relationship with the polis, with praxis, and with the slave/subaltern—in a manner that is different. Marx, Tagore, Heidegger, Arendt and Lacan remain symptomatic of such melancholic moments in philosophy's relationship with loss, with what it lost, perhaps in the Greek theatre.

Melancholy Gender

> ... The free libido was not displaced on to another object; it was withdrawn *into* the ego. There ... it served to establish an *identification* of the ego with the abandoned object. (Freud 1953: 159)

The urge and inspiration of this paper 'Melancholy Philosophy' comes from Butler's (1997: 132-150) understanding of gender *as* melancholic (identification) through a re-reading of 'Mourning and Melancholia' and *The Ego and the Id.* Butler shows how in both texts Freud argues that in melancholia an "object cathexis" is replaced by an "identification". Butler thus connects loss and identification. There is, as if, a compensatory over-identification with what has been lost (however, to designate gender as "melancholy" or for that matter, to designate philosophy "melancholy", one will have to take note of the three fundamental features of melancholia: loss and ego-splitting, loss and ambivalence, loss and ego-loss). Building on Freud, Butler argues that 'this kind of substitution [of loss by identification] has a great share in determining the form taken by the ego and that it makes an essential contribution toward building what is called its 'character':

> When it happens that a person has to give up a sexual object, there quite often ensues an alteration of his ego which can only be described as a setting up of the object *inside* the ego, as it occurs in melancholia ... "it may be that this identification is the sole condition under which the id can give up its objects ... the ego is a precipitate of abandoned object-cathexes". (1997: 133-34)

The architecture of the ego is marked by the 'sedimentation of objects loved and lost/abandoned'. The ego is an 'archaeological remainder' of past object-choices and of unresolved grief. Melancholy, is thus read by Butler, as the 'unfinished process of grieving' (however, the ego is not just a passive remainder; it is marked/scarred by a constant and painful reminder of things past, of things lost; it is a force-field of negative affect: there is splitting; there is ambivalence: i.e. the see-saw between doubled up wishes—love/hate, sadism masochism [Bose 1949]).

Butler shows how in *The Ego and the Id* Freud makes room for the notion that melancholic identification may be a *prerequisite* for letting the object go. There is thus no object-loss. There is rebound and exaggerated identification where identification becomes a magical, a psychic form of preserving the object (yes, but that serves as *anti-preservation* for the ego. The ego is, as if, eaten up by the identification: there is an auto-eating, an auto-cannibalism, an auto-thanato-graph). Insofar as identification is the psychic shadow, or psychic remainder of the object, 'the lost object continues to haunt and inhabit the ego as one of its constitutive identifications'. There is thus no complete loss or full abandonment of the object. There is just a transfer of the object from outside to inside, from an exteriorized entity to an interiorized shadow/trace. 'Giving up the object becomes possible only on the condition of a melancholic internalization or, what might for our purposes turn out to be even more important, a melancholic *incorporation*' and 'internalization will be a way to *disavow* the loss, to keep it at bay, to stay or postpone the recognition and suffering of loss'. (Butler 1997: 134)

> Gender [is] produced through melancholic identification. ... It seems clear that the positions of "masculine" and "feminine", which Freud in *Three Essays on the Theory of Sexuality* (1905) understood as the effects of laborious and uncertain accomplishment, are established in part through prohibitions which *demand the loss* of certain sexual attachments, and demand as well that those losses *not* be avowed, and *not* be grieved. If the assumption of femininity and the assumption of masculinity proceed through the accomplishment of an always tenuous heterosexuality, we might understand the force of this accomplishment as mandating the abandonment of homosexual attachments; or, perhaps more trenchantly, *preempting* the possibility of homosexual attachment, a foreclosure of possibility which produces a domain of homosexuality understood as *unlivable* passion and *ungrievable* loss. (Butler 1997: 135)

Butler moves between identification, internalization and incorporation, though she largely focuses on identification. I would, however, like to distinguish a little more closely among these three. Identification in psychoanalytic parlance is a process of getting assimilated into an aspect, property, or attribute of the Other.

Such assimilation into the traits of the Other transforms, wholly or partially, the self/subject (as is the case, perhaps, in melancholia, but only in a limited sense; this is because melancholia is not just about identification: all forms of identification do not render the subject melancholic). Personality is seen in psychoanalysis as a product of processes of identification. One identifies with Others or traits of significant Others early in childhood, which in turn shapes and constitutes personality. However, identification cannot be the only aspect of melancholia. In melancholia we shall have to account for the splitting or compartmentalization of the ego and the cocooning of the trace of the Other in one compartment of the ego, which functions as that part of the ego that "eats up" the other part: Hence the self-depreciation. Internalization, on the other hand, is constitutive of the formation of the "super-ego" function: internalization, say, of the Father's "no". Incorporation is a concept that Freud did not develop much. It was Abraham and Torok who developed the concept of incorporation through a close reading of the Wolf Man case in the context of the transmission of a (family) secret and the secret transmission of an intergenerational trauma, through "phantom effects". Incorporation, as distinguished from introjecton, is a *secret identification* with the Other. Crypt, the twin concept, is the *burial*, as I have shown above, of an *inadmissible* (as also inassimilable) identification—identification with an Other, an experience, more specifically a signifier. Incorporation and "crypt effect" as twin concepts (though different, as Derrida argues) gives an interesting twist to the melancholic('s) tale. In fact, the Freudian unconscious gets re-written, re-drawn, remapped as a *psychic crypt*; and a third path (Abraham and Torok 1986, 1994) gets inaugurated—beyond Freudianism and Lacanianism (Deleuze and Guattari inaugurate the fourth in *Anti-Oedipus*). Crypt is where the lost object is swallowed and preserved (my stress is on the preserved), like as "living dead". Crypt is also the place where the secrets and phantoms of the past are entombed or sepulchered. We have seen above how two interrelated processes constitute incorporation: "demetaphorization" and "objectivation" (Abraham and Torok 1994). Incorporation [thus] is 'the refusal to acknowledge the full import of the loss'. The question that this paper confronts, is, then, the following: which one is at work in philosophy and how? How do loss and identification, loss and incorporation, loss and ego-splitting, loss and ambivalence, loss and ego-loss work in philosophy? Where is the place for self-reproach or self-baratement in philosophy? How do they work? Do they? What is the place of family secrets in philosophy? What are the phantom effects and crypt effects? The next section is an exploration of the possibility of seeing (marginal) moments in philosophy—moments that are (a) at times, circulating around proper names: Socrates (through Arendt), Marx, Tagore, Heidegger Lacan, (b) at other times, circulating around concepts: *peithein*, *doxa*, *phronesis*, praxis, and (c) at yet other times, circulating as a register: the "slave's know-how"—as melancholic.

Melancholy Philosophy

> The free libido was not displaced on to another object; it was withdrawn *into* the ego. There ... it served to establish an *identification* of the ego with the abandoned object. Thus the *shadow* of the object fell upon the ego, and the latter could henceforth be judged by a special agency, as though it were an *object*, the forsaken object. In this way an *object-loss* was transformed into an *ego-loss,* and the conflict between the ego and the loved person into a cleavage between the critical activity of the ego and the ego as altered by identification (Freud 1953: 159).

This section of the paper is a presencing of moments of loss in the history of Western philosophy: loss of touch with the polis, loss of the perspective of praxis (and the consequent hyper-separation of thought and action) and phronesis (and the overemphasis on theoria, sophia or episteme), loss of contact with the slave and the slave's know-how. It is a foregrounding of how at times, in the work of some philosophers, actually a *few* philosophers (while most others moved on), the lost/loss was withdrawn into the philosophical ego; it is to ask: how the identification of the philosophical ego with the lost/loss nevertheless remained and continued to linger in some philosophers, and how such incorporated yet crypted loss rendered the philosophical ego self-reviling. This is the melancholy face(t) of philosophy. Melancholy philosophy is the minor chord of philosophy. Much of philosophy has mourned such loss and has moved on with renewed vigor to substitute objects. Only a few have continued to be melancholic. One is Arendt.

The Abyss Between Thought and Action

Arendt (2005: 6) introduces a decisive wedge between Socrates and Plato. She shows how this wedge produced an "abyss"—an abyss more serious, perhaps, than the wedge—an abyss, which 'immediately opened between thought and action, and which never since has been closed'[8]. Marx, Tagore and Heidegger return to this abyss between thought and action. These thinkers remain haunted by this originary loss, by the loss of the perspective of action in philosophy. For all three (especially Marx and Tagore) this loss (the trace of which is cocooned and crypted in their philosophical ego), led in turn to a self-reproach and self-beratement. While much of philosophy had mourned this loss and had moved on to compensatory overdrive around thought, Marx, Tagore and Heidegger remain melancholic about this loss. They find their philosophical egos haunted by this loss, by philosophy's loss of libido for action, practice, and labor. Philosophy's family secret had phantom effects on their work and corpus.

Praxis

Marx shows in the first of the eleven *Theses on Feuerbach* how in *The Essence of Christianity* [*Das Wesen des Christenthums*] Feuerbach 'regards the theoretical attitude as the only genuinely human attitude, while practice [*Praxis*] is conceived and defined only in its dirty-Jewish form of appearance [*Erscheinungsform*]. Hence he does not grasp the significance of 'revolutionary', of 'practical-critical', activity (Marx 2002 [1845]).[9] Why, however, is practice Jewish? Why is practice dirty? Here Marx (footnote 1 by Smith and Cuckson) looks to be guided by an interesting distinction—a distinction that looks to have been missed in the hyper-secular rhetoric of most Marxists—between the Christian discourse on creation and the Judaic discourse on creation. Smith and Cuckson quote Marshall Berman to argue that "dirty-Jewish" is possibly 'an allusion to the Jewish God of the Old Testament', who had to 'get his hands dirty' while creating the world, and is tied up with a 'symbolic contrast between the Christian God of the Word, and the God of the Deed, symbolizing practical life' (Marx 2002, footnote 1). This distinct marking of the Deed as against the "dead" (i.e., dead or inert matter), in sharp contradistinction to Feuerbach, is key to the Marxian perspective on materialism. Marx is thus making a distinction not just between the "real" and the "speculative, " between matter and idea, materialism and idealism, but also between the mere Word and the Deed—which is why Marx (2002) feels that the 'dispute over the reality or unreality of thinking' is a 'practical question' and 'it is in practice [in Deed, indeed] that man must prove the truth'.

While Marx remains melancholic about the lost perspective of praxis in philosophy, Tagore remains melancholic about the lost perspective of the praxical nature of thought. For Tagore it is the praxical ground of thought that births the being's world; it is the praxical substratum that births the being's ways of being in the world.

> Our *tapovanas*, which were our natural Universities were not abstracted from *life*[10] ... and the spiritual education, which the students had, was a part of the spiritual life itself which comprehended all life. ... ... Such an institution must group round it all the neighbouring villages and virtually unite them with itself in all its economic endeavours. ... In a word, it should never be like a meteor—only a stray fragment of a world—but a complete world in itself ... . (Tagore 2011: 160)

Tagore tries to return in *Shantiniketan* (the abode of peace) and thereafter in *Sriniketan* (the abode of the aesthetic) to the coordinated experience of brain and hand in the everyday life-world of school going children.

> When the time comes for our thinkers and intellectuals to take agricultural activities under their responsibility, the schism that at present exists between the hand and the brain ... will vanish. (Tagore 2011: 139)

Tagore remains haunted by the lost perspective of praxis; praxis as the foreclosed of the University imagination—an imagination steeped in and limited to the learning, teaching, writing of the cognitivist sciences. While the classical imagination of the University sharpened largely the cognitive and the intellectual self, Tagore inaugurated in the 'culture of the self', the creative expression and praxis of the affective, the aesthetic, and the ethical; the praxis of being-in-the-world which is "disclosed" and being-with-nature; the praxis of labouring activities in the "average everydayness" of the *ashram*; the praxis of self- and social transformation. Tagore's turn to *Shantiniketan* and *Sriniketan* could be seen as a departure from the classical university imagination and from the kind of cognitivist student subject the University mass-produces. Such mass production of cognitive student subjects in turn creates a culture of *turning away* from the (laboring) masses (or as Arendt suggests: the *polis*; or as Lacan suggests: the slave and the slave's know-how); more on the history of this loss in the context of the birth of Western philosophy in Plato's dialogues below (Lacan 2007).

Phronesis

If Marx and Tagore were melancholic about the lost perspective of praxis, Heidegger (1985, 1997) was melancholic about the lost perspective of phronesis. In 1923 at the University of Freiburg, Heidegger delivered a seminar on the Aristotelian concept (invoked in Book 4 of the *Nichomachean Ethics*) of phronesis—phronesis as distinct from "sophia" and "episteme"; phronesis as the "other reason" or the other (way to) *truth*; phronesis as pointing to 'the possibility of developing a critically self-reflective model of ontological knowledge' firmly embedded in the finite *world* (Heidegger 1985: 59-61) and in *life*[11]; phronesis as being-related to the *with-which*. What is phronesis? In one sense, practical[12] reason, as distinct from theoretical reason. In another sense, it is reasoning based on concrete practical action, as distinct from speculative reason. In yet another but related sense, it is reason based on experience as distinct from abstract deductions. Phronesis is thus 'a form of knowledge capable of critically considering [i.e., reflecting upon] the conditions of its own operation' (Long 2002: 36). Where sophia seeks 'eternal certainty' (i.e. *what cannot be otherwise*), phronesis settles for the 'contingent existence of human beings' (i.e. *what can be otherwise*) and works with 'dynamic, contingent principles endemic to ethics' (Ibid: 37); where sophia posits the absolute authority of 'first principles', phronesis identifies the concrete encounter with the other qua other as the ultimate ground for truth; where sophia demeans 'being-related to the with-which', phronesis affirms its fundamental significance as a determining condition for truth. An ontology directed by phronesis rather than sophia would not seek refuge in the realm of 'universal knowledge' but would recognize its own inherent embeddedness in the world of praxis and being-related, and would thus be capable of critically considering the historico-ethico-political conditions under which it is deployed (also Bowler 2008).

Carr shows how 'within the dominant culture of modernity, the concepts of phronesis[13] and praxis have been rendered marginal and now face something approaching total obliteration' (2006: 434) and how *practical philosophy* is now largely a lost tradition (Gadamer 1980). Taking off once again from Aristotle in *The Nicomachean Ethics* (1955), Carr makes the distinction, not between sophia/episteme and phronesis but between *poiesis* and praxis: 'poiesis refers to the numerous *productive* activities that form the basis of economic life. Since it is a form of 'making action' whose end is known prior to the practical means taken to achieve it, poiesis is guided by the form of reasoning that the Greeks called *techne* and that we would today call instrumental 'means-end' reasoning. Poiesis is thus a form of instrumental action that requires a mastery of the knowledge, methods and skills that together constitute technical expertise. For the Greeks, the activities of craftsmen and artisans were paradigm cases of *poiesis* guided by *techne*. And, as such, they were guided by 'productive philosophy'—what we would today call 'applied science'—which provide the principles, procedures and operational methods which together constitute the most effective means for achieving some predetermined end' (Carr 2006: 426). Praxis, on the other hand, is to progressively realize the idea of the "good" that is constitutive of a morally worthwhile form of human life; the "end" of praxis hence is not to *make* or produce some object or artifact. The good of praxis, however, cannot be "made": it can only be "done". Praxis is thus a form of "doing" action precisely because its "end"—to arrive at good life—'*only* exists, and can *only* be realized, *in and through* praxis *itself*' (Carr 2006: 426). 'Praxis also differs from poiesis in that knowledge of its end cannot be theoretically specified in advance and can only be acquired on the basis of an understanding of how, in a particular concrete situation, this knowledge is being interpreted and applied. Praxis is thus nothing other than a practical manifestation of how the idea of the good is being understood, just as knowledge of the good is nothing other than an abstract way of specifying the mode of human conduct through which this idea is given practical expression. In praxis, acquiring knowledge of what the good is and knowing how to apply it in particular situations are thus not two separate processes but two mutually supportive constitutive elements within a single dialectical process of practical reasoning' (Carr 2006: 426; Dunne 1993).

Carr remains haunted by the lost perspective of phronesis (as against thought as *theoria*) and praxis (as against action as poiesis). Entombed in the "abyss of thought and action" are two losses: loss of the perspective of phronesis and of praxis; both losses continue to haunt philosophy and render Marxian, Tagorite or Heideggerian philosophy melancholic.

The Loss of the Relation with the Polis

If the abyss between thought and action and the loss of the perspective of action is one, the other is what Arendt (2005: 6) designates as 'the gulf between philosophy and politics opened historically with the trial and condemnation of Socrates, which in the history of political thought plays the same role of a turning point that the trial and condemnation of Jesus plays in the history of religion':

> ... the death of Socrates made Plato despair of polis life and, at the same time, doubt certain fundamentals of Socrates' teachings. The fact that Socrates had not been able to persuade his judges of his innocence and his merits, which were so obvious to the better and younger of Athens' citizens, made Plato doubt the validity of *persuasion*. ... "Persuasion" is a very weak and inadequate translation of the ancient *peithein,* the political importance of which is indicated by the fact that Peitho, the goddess of persuasion, had a temple in Athens. To persuade, *peithein,* was the specifically political form of speech, and since the Athenians were proud that they, in distinction to the barbarians, conducted their political affairs in the form of speech and without compulsion, they considered rhetoric, the art of persuasion, the highest, the truly political art. (Arendt 2005: 6-7)

Arendt shows how Plato's 'doubt about the validity of persuasion' was supplemented by Plato's 'furious denunciation of *doxa,* opinion'.[14] This led to Plato's 'despair of polis life' or 'life in the polis' or the 'philosopher's life in the polis, tied to the polis, to life in the polis, to polis life. It came at a cost, a deadly cost: death; and with the death of Socrates came the death of the philosophic-political praxis of being-in-the-polis'. Socrates had tried to make philosophy relevant to the polis; or the polis relevant to philosophy. But philosophy ended in *apolitia,* the 'indifference and contempt for the world of the city, so characteristic of all post-Platonic philosophy'; as if, the philosopher had to protect himself or herself from the world around; as if, being in the world was detrimental to the sacred task of philosophizing about the world. Arendt (2005) shows how with Aristotle the time begins when philosophers no longer feel responsible for the city, and this not only in the sense that philosophy has no special task in the realm of politics, but in the much larger sense that the philosopher has less responsibility for it than any of his fellow citizens, that the philosopher's way of life is different. There was consensus about the inherent incompatibility between the fundamental philosophical and the fundamental political experiences: 'The Socratic position was lost in this process, not because Socrates did not leave any writings behind or because Plato willfully distorted him, but because the Socratic insights, born out of a still-intact relationship between politics and the specifically philosophical experience, was lost' (Arendt 2005: 36). Melancholic Marx, melancholic about philosophy's lost touch with the polis and the political, engender the rebirthing of the Socratic moment.

The Loss of the Slave's Know-How

Tagore's critique (2011; also see above) of the classical university imagination and of the cognitivist perspective (Tagore's writings and Tagore's actions—i.e. Tagore's *turning away* from the kind of *parrot's training* Universities impart and the creation of *Shantiniketan* for practices of self-transformation through the realization of creative freedom and *Sriniketan* for practices of social transformation through "rural reconstruction"—stand testimony to such a critique) finds a somewhat surprising ally in Lacan (2007: 11-26). Lacan speaks, however, of a Discourse of the University. Lacan, unlike Foucault, talks of only Four Discourses though: the Discourse of the University, the Master's Discourse, the Hysteric's Discourse, and the Analyst's Discourse. Discourse is for Lacan the structure of a 'fundamental relation' 'of one signifier to another' and from this relation emerges what Lacan calls "the subject" (Lacan 2007: 13). And all four discourses revolve around a fundamental impossibility: of education, of mastery, of 'inciting of desire', and of analysis. In each Discourse, a *truth* drives the *agent*, the agent addresses the *Other*, leading to a *product*. But the position of truth, agent, Other and product can be occupied by any one of the "four terms": 'master signifier', 'Knowledge', 'object petit *a*' and 'divided subject'.

$$\uparrow \frac{\text{Agent}}{\text{Truth}} \rightarrow \frac{\text{Other}}{\text{Product}} \downarrow$$

Four terms:
master signifier (S_1)
Knowledge (S_2)
objet petit a (*a*)
divided subject ($\$$)

University Discourse

$$\frac{S_2}{S_1} \rightarrow \frac{a}{\$}$$

Master's Discourse

$$\frac{S_1}{\$} \rightarrow \frac{S_2}{a}$$

Hysteric's Discourse

$$\frac{\$}{a} \rightarrow \frac{S_1}{S_2}$$

Analyst's Discourse

$$\frac{a}{S_2} \rightarrow \frac{\$}{S_1}$$

Let us discuss the Discourse of the Master; all the more because the Discourse of the University, contrary to all expectation, appears to be apposite to and not the opposite of the Master's Discourse. The Discourse of the Master can be seen in the master-slave relation (Lacan 2007: 29-32) or in authoritarianism where a 'master signifier' standing in for the master/dictator issues orders. In the Discourse of the Master, a master/dictator would speak from the position of agent unaware of its *own* vulnerability. Let us now move to the Discourse of the University and its relationship with the Master's Discourse; a quarter turn in the anti-clockwise direction takes the Master's Discourse to the Discourse of the University; where the master signifier is 'unconscious original knowledge' that supports the knowledge that is to be taught in the classroom context, and the knowledge that is to be taught is addressed to the student-lacking-in-knowledge. The Discourse of the University, according to Lacan, is the secret rationalization of the Master's Discourse. It is the delusional veil of knowledge over the master's lack of discourse; the Discourse of the University covers the master's lack (Lacan 2007: 41). Lacan's (2007 [1969-1970]) enumeration of the Discourse of the University *on the side* of the Master's Discourse comes as a surprise. We were expecting the Discourse of the University to be *on the other side* of the Master's Discourse, to be on the side of the lived experience and discourse of the "slave"; the University looked to be aligned with the world of the "slave". It is in this context, that Lacan foregrounds the 'theft, abduction, stealing slavery of its knowledge [transference, plundering, spoliation of what, at the beginning of knowledge, was inscribed, hidden, in the slave's world] through the maneuvers of the master' in Plato's dialogues (Lacan 2007: 21, 34, 38, 51, 79). The entire function of the *episteme* as 'transmissible knowledge' is borrowed from the techniques of the craftsmen, of the serfs, of women working in households: 'It is a matter of extracting the essence of this [community] knowledge in order for it to become the master's knowledge', or 'theoretical knowledge'—theoretical knowledge in the emphatic sense that the word "theoria" has in Aristotle, or has in Hegel with respect to "absolute knowledge" (Lacan 2007: 22). Lacan referred to *Meno* in saying that Socrates intervened as the Master in order to convert the know-how of the slave into a transmissible *episteme,* that is, the knowledge of the *geometry* (Lacan 2007: 22-23). Lacan is also concerned about the 'persistence of a master's discourse', about what happens between the classical and coercive Master's Discourse and that of the modern secular subtle master—the consent generating University—is a modification in the place of knowledge: this is how knowledge becomes theoretical and cognitive. The western philosophical tradition 'has some responsibility of this transmutation' (Lacan 2007: 31). 'Philosophy in its historical function is this *extraction*, of the slave's knowledge [for Lacan, and of the woman's knowledge for Irigaray], in order to obtain its transmutation into the master's knowledge' (Lacan 2007: 22).

> In Antiquity this was not simply a class, as with our modern slave, it was a *function* inscribed in the family. The slave Aristotle speaks of is just as much a part of the family as he is a part of the State, and even more a part of the family than a part of the State. This is because he is the one who has the know-how *(savoir-faire).* Before we can know whether the knowledge is known, whether a subject can be founded on the perspective of a knowledge that is tot ally transparent in itself, it is important to know how to mop

> up the register of what, at its origins, know-how is. Now, what is it that happens right before our very eyes, which gives meaning, an initial meaning—as you will see, there are other meanings—to philosophy? Fortunately we have traces of this thanks to Plato, and it is quite essential to remember this so as to put what is at issue in its place and, after all, if anything in what is bothering us has any sense, it can only come from putting things in their place. What does philosophy designate over its entire evolution? It's this-theft, abduction, stealing slavery of its knowledge, through the maneuvers of the master. To see this it is enough to read Plato's dialogues ... I begin by distinguishing what on this occasion I will call the two aspects of knowledge, the *articulated aspect* and this know-how akin to animal knowledge. but which in the slave is not totally devoid of the apparatus that transforms it into one of the most articulated networks of language. The point is that this, the second layer, the articulated apparatus can be transmitted, which means it can be transmitted from the slave's pocket to the master's—as summing they had pockets in those days. It is here that you have the entire effort to isolate what is called *episteme.* (Lacan, 2007: 21-22)

Lacan uncorks the master's discourse, and what one gets is the University Discourse. University Discourse is the 'new tyranny of knowledge', as the (modern secular) sieve through which we are on the whole all recruited. The dominant position in the University Discourse is occupied by theoretical and cognitive knowledge. This illustrates the fact that behind all attempts to impart an apparently "neutral" knowledge, one can see an attempt at mastery (mastery of knowledge, and domination of the Other to whom this knowledge is imparted). Lacan hence asserts: 'Who can deny that philosophy has ever been anything other than a fascinating enterprise for the master's benefit?' (Dolar 2006).[15] The translation of the slave's know-how into the master's theoria is a moment of loss for Lacan: it is a loss that in turn haunts Lacan's philosophy. Lacan's 'anti-philosophy' is not a position against philosophy; it is the melancholic side of philosophy, it is the Other Side of Philosophy.

It is when philosophy *touches* melancholy[16], it's own, as also ours, our collective melancholy, that philosophy becomes a *touching exercise.*

Notes

1. While 'the ego probably succumbs in melancholia', in mania 'it has overcome it or pushed it aside' (Freud 2006).
2. The inspiration of this paper comes from the late Lacan's (1969-70) attempts to move to *The Other Side of Psychoanalysis* (2007): the move to the *Other Side* is the move to *the* side psychoanalysis has been melancholic about. It is the move to the *Other Side* of "case histories", or what in psychiatrized or psychologized psychoanalysis is called "clinical"; move to what psychoanalysis remains melancholic about: the lost "social", the absent "political"; it is the move to the side of the Four Discourses: 'discourse without speech' (Lacan 2007: 12), the move to 'a *revival* [of psychoanalysis] *from the other direction*' (Lacan 2007: 12): the non-clinical, the non-dyadic, the non-Oedipalized direction. Taking off from Lacan this paper asks: what is it to move to *The Other Side of Philosophy*, to the side philosophy is melancholic about?
3. Freud, Sigmund (1917), 'Trauer und Melancholie' [Mourning and Melancholia] in *Internationale Zeitschrift für Ärztliche Psychoanalyse* (in German). Leipzig and Vienna: Hugo Heller. 4 (6): 288–301. The German '*Trauer*', like the English 'mourning', can mean both the *affect of grief* and its *outward manifestation.*
4. Freud also talks of a third response in the same piece: 'a turning away from reality takes place and a clinging to the object through the medium of a hallucinatory wishful psychosis'. However, 'normally, respect for reality gains the day' and the subject ends up acknowledging and mourning the lost/loss.
5. Žižek (2000) however argues that melancholia occurs not when we *lose* the object, but rather when we no longer *desire* it. It is the *lack* of desire, not the loss of the object that makes one melancholic. It is lack of desire that complicates the relationship of the subject to the object; it is the lack of desire that renders the object quasi-lost to the subject. In this reading, reading from the pole of desire (i.e. reading from the psychoanalytic angle) and not from the pole of loss (i.e. reading from the historical, more evental angle), it is the subject who has lost (desire for) the object; it is not the object that has abandoned the subject; it is desire that has abandoned the subject. The question then is not *who* is lost but *what* is lost. It is desire that is lost. The subject has lost desire (for the object). It is not the object but the *object cause of desire* that is lost (melancholia is, as if, *premature mourning* for an object before it is lost [see https://cengizerdem.wordpress.com/2013/01/27/melancholia-and-the-cartesian-subject/]). Freud writes in *Mourning and Melancholia*: 'The object has not perhaps actually died, but has been lost as an object of love (e.g. in the case of a betrothed girl who has been jilted)'. One can read 'lost as an object of love' in at least two ways: one, where the subject has lost the object; two, where the subject has lost love for the object, i.e. where the object is no more the object of love. The question the paper asks: has philosophy lost desire for the Socratic moment of being-in-the-polis, for being in touch with praxis, with phronesis, with the slave and the

slave's know-how? Has contemporary philosophy lost desire for the 'pre-modern tradition of 'practical philosophy'—a tradition that permeated Western intellectual culture until the seventeenth century and that has only been finally discarded in our own modern times' (Toulmin 1988).

6. Object loss 'does not mean that the loved object has died or gone away or been unfaithful, though any of these may have been the precipitating event that created the danger of the loss of the object, and though psychologically any and all these things may have happened. Object loss means that something catastrophic has happened to the subject's *internal connection* with his object' (Roth in Fiorini, Bokanowski and Lewkowicz 2009: 38). This takes us back to Žižek (2000) and the question the paper asks: did something catastrophic happen in the transition from Socrates to Plato? Did philosophy lose its "internal connection" with the polis, with life in the polis? Did philosophy lose its connection with praxis, with phronesis, with the slave and with the slave's know-how?
7. 'Incorporation denotes a fantasy, introjection a process'. Two interrelated processes constitute incorporation: 'demetaphorization (taking literally what is meant figuratively)' and 'objectivation (pretending that the suffering is not an injury to the subject but instead a loss sustained by the love object)' … incorporation [thus] is the refusal to acknowledge the full import of the loss.' Introjection, on the other hand, is the process of 'broadening the ego' through 'transferential love' (Abraham and Torok 1994).
8. 'All thinking activity that is not simply the calculation of means to obtain an intended or willed end, but is concerned with meaning in the most general sense, came to play the role of an "afterthought, " that is, after action had decided and determined reality. Action, on the other hand, was relegated to the meaningless realm of the accidental and haphazard' (Arendt 2005: 6).
9. *Theses on Feuerbach* was written by Marx in Brussels in the spring of 1845. Marx's original text was first published in 1924. The English translation was first published in *The German Ideology* in 1938. The version I am quoting has been translated by Cyril Smith in 2002 and is based on work done jointly with Don Cuckson (https://www.marxists.org/archive/marx/works/1845/theses/).
10. '… the thrust of Heidegger's critique is not that previous philosophies had simply failed to grasp life, although that surely happened, but that previous philosophies presuppose life and also the living character of philosophy itself. In essence, their failure to grasp life in and for itself is due to the fact that life is always already present in the background of their philosophy'. However, 'what is at stake for Heidegger is not whether philosophy can or cannot give us access to life and lived-experience [in a radically new, pre-objective, pre-theoretical way], but rather to understand how philosophy itself is lived and situated in life. … previous attempts to grasp life philosophically failed because philosophy itself had become divorced from life and therefore the attempt to approach life philosophically was an artificial effort to grasp life 'from outside'. … this required retracing the way in which philosophy becomes alienated from life' (Bowler 2008: 2-6 and 116-137). Thus if Heidegger was trying to resituate philosophy in life, Tagore was

trying to resituate the experience of education in "spiritual life" which in turn "comprehended all life".

11. 'The *aletheia of phronesis* is living itself'; for Heidegger, 'philosophy is the intensification of life. It is, he argues, *philosophizing*. And philosophizing is just a pre-eminent form of *the praxis* of life' (Bowler 2008: 135-136).
12. '"Practical" behavior is not "atheoretical" in the sense of sightlessness [i.e. a lack of seeing]. The way it differs from theoretical behavior does not lie simply in the fact that in theoretical behavior one observes, while in practical behavior one *acts* [*gehandelt* wird], and that action must apply theoretical cognition if it is not to remain blind; for the fact that observation is a kind of concern [or taking care] is just as primordial as the fact that action has *its own* kind of sight [seeing] (Heidegger 1985: 99).
13. Dhar and Chakrabarti highlight Heidegger's turn to *phronesis* and his turning away from *episteme* or *sophia* (2016: 572-574).
14. 'The opposition of truth and opinion was certainly the most anti-Socratic conclusion that Plato drew from Socrates' trial' (Arendt 2005: 8).
15. Mladen Dolar, in "Hegel as the Other Side of Psychoanalysis", explores 'the *multiple* place that Hegel occupies in the four discourses'. Hegel at once *functions* 'as a representative of the master's, the hysteric's, and the university discourse, and, ultimately, can be seen to occupy the analyst's place as *objet a* as well' (Clemens and Grigg 2006: 5). Lacan argues: "at the level of the master's discourse something appeared which is of interest to us concerning discourse, irrespective of its ambiguity, and which is called *philosophy*" (Lacan 2007: 20).
16. The MPhil programme in Development *Practice* (*not* Studies) at Ambedkar University Delhi is an attempt—small albeit—at turning to polis-praxis-phronesis and the slave's know-how, and being in touch with the Other side of philosophy, the melancholic side.

References

Abraham, Nicolas and Maria Torok, *The Wolf Man's Magic Word: A Cryptonymy*, trans. Nicholas Rand (Minneapolis: University of Minnesota Press, 1986).

Abraham, Nicolas and Maria Torok, *The Shell and the Kernel: Renewals of Psychoanalysis*, Vol. 1, Ed. with an Introduction by Nicholas T. Rand (New York: University of Chicago Press, 1994).

Aristotle, *The Nicomachean Ethics*, trans. J.A.K. Thompson (London: Penguin, 1955).

Arendt, Hannah, *The Promise of Politics,* ed. with an Introduction by Jerome Kohn (New York: Schocken Books, 2005).

Bose, Girindrasekhar, *Concept of Repression* (Calcutta: Sri Gauranga Press and London: Kegan Paul, Trench, Troubner and Co., 1921).

Bose, Girindrasekhar, 'A New Theory of Mental Life' in *Samiksha*, Vol 2, No 2 (1948), http://www.samiksha.cuspthejournal.com/default.html.

Bose, Girindrasekhar, 'Ambivalence' in *Samiksha*, Vol 3, No 2 (1949), http://www.samiksha.cuspthejournal.com/default.html.

Bose, Girindrasekhar, 'The Nature of the Wish' in *Samiksha*, Vol 5, No 4 (1951), http://www.samiksha.cuspthejournal.com/default.html.

Bose, Girindrasekhar, 'Analysis of Wish' in *Samiksha*, Vol 6, No 1 (1952), http://www.samiksha.cuspthejournal.com/default.html.

Bowler, Michael, *Heidegger and Aristotle: Philosophy as Praxis* (New York and London: Continuum, 2008).

Carr, Wilfred, 'Philosophy, Methodology and Action Research' in *Journal of the Philosophy of Education* (Oxford and MA: Blackwell Publishing, 2006).

Clemens, Justin and Russell Grigg (ed.), *Reflections on Seminar XVII: Jacques Lacan and the Other Side of Psychoanalysis* (London: Duke University Press, 2006).

Dhar, Anup and Anjan Chakrabarti, 'Marxism as Ascetic: Spiritual as Phronetic' in *Rethinking Marxism*, Vol. 29, No 1, October (New York and London: Routledge, 2016), 563-583.

Dolar, Martin, 'Hegel and the Other Side of Psychoanalysis' in *Reflections on Seminar XVII: Jacques Lacan and the Other Side of Psychoanalysis,* eds. Justin Clemens and Russell Grigg (London: Duke University Press, 2006), 129-154.

Dunne, Joseph, *Back to the Rough Ground: 'Phronesis' and 'Techne' in Modern Philosophy and in Aristotle* (London: University of Notre Dame Press, 1993).

Freud, Sigmund, 'Trauer und Melancholie' in *Internationale Zeitschrift für Ärztliche Psychoanalyse* (in German). Leipzig and Vienna: Hugo Heller. 4 (6): 288–301; translated as 'Mourning and Melancholia' in *Sigmund Freud Collected Papers,* Volume 4. (London: Hogarth Press and the Institute of Psychoanalysis, 1953 [1917]), 152-172.

Gadamer, Hans-Georg, 'Practical Philosophy as a Model of the Human Sciences' in *Research in Phenomenology*, 9 (1980), 74–85.

Heidegger, Martin, *Being and Time,* trans. J. Macquarrie and E. Robinson (Oxford: Basil Blackwell, 1985 [1962]).

Heidegger, Martin, *Plato's Sophist,* trans. Richard Rojcewicz and André Schuwer (Bloomington: Indiana University Press, 1997).

Irigaray, Luce, *This Sex Which Is Not One,* trans. Catherine Porter (New York: Cornell University Press, 1985).

Lacan, Jacques, *Television: A Challenge to the Psychoanalytic Establishment,* ed. Joan Copjec (New York: W.W. Norton & Company, 1990).

Lacan, Jacques, *The Seminar of Jacques Lacan—The Other Side of Psychoanalysis—Book XVII,* ed. Jacques-Alain Miller and trans. with notes by Russell Grigg (New York and London: W.W. Norton & Company, 2007).

Long, Chistopher. P., 'The Ontological Reappropriation of Phronesis' in *Continental Philosophy Review* (2002), 35 (1): 35–60.

Marx, Karl, 'Theses on Feuerbach', trans. C. Smith (2002) (Marxists Internet Archive. Accessed 7 September, 2017. https://www.marxists.org/archive/marx/works/1845/theses/).

Miller, Jacques-Alain, 'Depression' in *Lacanian Ink* 31, trans. Thelma Sowley (2007).

Roth, Priscilla, 'Melancholia, Mourning, and the Countertransference' in *On Freud's "Mourning and Melancholia",* Contemporary Freud: Turning Points and Critical Issues, eds. Leticia Glocer Fiorini, Thierry Bokanowski, and Sergio Lewkowicz (London: Karnac Books, 2009), 37-55.

Skriabine, Pierre, 'Some Moral Failings Called Depressions', trans. Jack Stone, www.lacan.com in *The Symptom* Issue 1 (1997).

Tagore, Rabindranath, *The Oxford India Tagore: Selected Writings on Education and Nationalism,* ed. Uma Dasgupta (Oxford: New Delhi, 2011).

Toulmin, Stephen, 'The Recovery of Practical Philosophy' in *The American Scholar* (1988), 57.3, p. 354.

Žižek, Slavoj, 'Melancholy and the Act' in *Critical Inquiry* (2000), 26.4, 657-81.

Reimagining the 'Loss' and Reinventing the Space
The Dialectics of European Melancholy

Krishnan Unni P

Contesting Factors

The concept of melancholy has always been perceived as one of the endless paradigmatic connotations in Europe since the beginning of the 20th century. Apart from several socio- historical features that turned the shape of melancholy, the notion called "melancholia" was something deeply ridden in the personal quest for identity, transformation of the self into special strata of its own and the idea of interiorizing the world in terms of acute inward looking questions. The common features of melancholy, therefore, varied in their intensity and the modes of a certain ethical stance that offered both a sense of comfort and desolation at times. One of the major popularly known assumptions of melancholy was its relation to loneliness—both as a pathological syndrome and psychological. This, we must understand, was a difficult construct that went along with the struggles of modernism in Europe. Sigmund Freud's celebrated text 'Mourning and Melancholia' as well as his other psychological detailing of the lives of persons, needless to say, opened up a question of melancholy in a different way. The question of loneliness here became a special mode of observance: the lone person who suffers from a certain psychological condition began to get transform herself/himself into an object of observation. Sidelining the historical and philosophical assumptions of melancholy, the idea of loneliness connected to psychological malaise used to be considered as the chief modality of modern melancholy. A number of Freudian disciples including Carl Gustav Jung, R.D. Laing and later William Reich found problems with this condition. However, this condition of modernity gradually created a fissure in the intellectual history of Europe. This fissure needs to be understood from the perspective of how to view the modern subject, which undergoes melancholy and the ways in which melancholy intersected the historical and political dimensions of modern life. What we see here is an interesting trajectory of Freud's psychoanalysis getting astutely overburdened by a series of internal discourses and the challenge against one type of an individuation and subject formation.

The nexus between love and loss figured as the primary corpus of Freudian melancholy. This in many senses was not considered as the chief constituent of the formation of the modern subject. Yet there were tendencies that made this idea the core of the subject formation in modernism. In 'Mourning and Melancholia', Freud observes: 'In one class of cases it is evident that melancholia too may be the reaction to the loss of a loved object. Where this is not the exciting cause one can perceive that there is a loss of a more ideal kind. The object has not perhaps actually died, but has become lost as an object of love..... In yet other cases, one feels justified in concluding that a loss of the kind has been experienced, but one cannot see clearly what has been lost, and may the more readily suppose that the patient too cannot consciously perceive what it is he has lost' (1986: 245). It is evident from this statement that Freud was planning to create a systemic attention to the object, which is perceived as the object of love and the sense of loss of the individual. This much appreciated stance of Freud becomes problematic when we look at the subject devoid of its strangeness or proximity to the object as a separate entity. This also raises certain questions about the validity of the object and the kind of love that is attributed to the object. It is ironic that this Freudian object is misunderstood as the 'other' or the opposite sex by several scholars and critics. If we follow this to be true, we need to surmise that depression turns out to be an aberrant form of mourning. However, the cause of mourning can be quite different other than this fixed psychological malaise. The subject, often understood as the "in- between" character, can never be fixed on a certain platform of such psychological conditions. Though the resistance against the Freudian idea of mourning became sharper in the post war years, many of them also slipped into the terrain of a Freudian groundwork of situating the subject versus object condition. Given the fact that the modern subject is a divided one, one needs to look at the other ramifications of adducing a singularity in terms of Freudian psychoanalysis to outline certain conditions of socio-historical conflicts of melancholy.

While Freud's understanding of melancholy was centered on the world of the depressive and the narcissistic regression that follows, the notion of the libidinal investment remained untheorized in his theoretical formulation. What can be the ways by which the subject of melancholy transfers her/his libidinal investment to the ego? Can the ego function in an atmosphere where such desires are only invested without any outlet? Can the ego be considered as the perfect exemplum of melancholy? These questions remain still unanswered in the wider debates of European modernism. Julia Kristeva answers some of these queries, if not in a positive way, but by situating the question of desire, stating that melancholy marks the 'impossible mourning' (Kristeva 1992: 14-15). The stress on the "impossible" needs to be noted specifically. This "impossible mourning" is intended for the presymbolic "Thing". The question of language here becomes very important. For Kristeva, every melancholic invariably strives to guard the lost treasure. In order to guard this treasure she/he stores it in the *a*symbolic realm of the Real, which rejects the language and any other specifications of the unnameable or untraceable "Thing" that words seek to occupy. For example, a modern subject under melancholy essentially turns out to be the one that rejects the language of experiments and communication and delves deep into a system of other significations to retain the proximity of the pre-symbolic "Thing". The "Thing" Kristeva talks about is no more a particular subject or an object of desire. Moreover, it has certain definite connotations to a system of asymmetric layers of pre-language formation. Thus, it is by an involvement with the pre-symbolic and with the rejection of the language; the melancholic finds its expression in society.

Kristeva's psychoanalytic stance is considered as the post-Lacanian phase of understanding melancholy and desire. However, what is significant here is not the fact that the rejection of the language of the subject and the consequent rise of the pre-symbolic world; on the other hand, the involvement of the subject in a chain of significations which, more than in any language formation functions as the antidote of Freudian depression. One should not misunderstand that Kristeva was articulating an idea of silence or, a passage to that by claiming that subject has not lost anything. The subjects' critical stance here is the most palpable and predicative one as it is forced to stand between the loss that is understood pre-symbolically and the difficulty to recuperate the loss. Melancholy as a philosophic discourse or as a language that further attests the human potentialities is not clearly evident in Kristeva's argument. While the modern subject is perceived as the one far too removed from staticity and often conceived as a divided one, this psychoanalytic stance distanced the same from systemic interpretations. The stress on the subject and its association with the multiplicities is what perhaps may be counted as the internal dichotomy of the discourse of melancholy in the European context. Andre Green further elaborates this by analyzing Kristeva's ideas. He states that the role of the psychic apparatus lies in 'supplying content to what is experienced only in an unrepresentable form' (Green 1986: 211). Green's suggestion makes it clear that more than the psychoanalytic therapy, the prelinguistic displacement of energy can be possible as the subject wavers from one extreme to the other. The task of the modern subject, therefore, seems to situate itself with some sense of autonomy. This is where the ways of interpreting melancholy becomes problematic.

Melancholy's distinctive turn in the 20th century—its moving away from both the psychological and overtly seen pathological social condition—is developed by Walter Benjamin. In his early works of Benjamin, one can find the influence of the Talmudic tradition and other Jewish influences. Melancholy attains significant roles in Benjamin's philosophic and aesthetic thoughts. More than a psycho-social malaise often attributed to the modern subject, in Benjamin's writings melancholy turns out to be a stance that would bring forth some ethical and moral responsibility to the other and it functions often as a linguistic disclosure of the world. The so far seen modern subject, far from its internal divisions and contradictions is seen here as a positive dynamism that would encapsulate the different strands of melancholy. In the early works of Benjamin, particularly those that deal with his writings of student days and later culminating with *The Origin of German Tragic Drama*, melancholy is seen as attunement. The opening up of the divine and the mortal conflates the attunement (*Stimmung*) many times. As it is provided in the Judeo- Christian traditions, the fundamental stake here is the way in which human beings can bring this *Stimmung* among the many possibilities and distancing of/from certain responsibilities. The inextricable link between melancholy and philosophy lies in a series of attunements that would suffice the ethics of human beings.

It is often misunderstood that Benjamin developed the idea of melancholy out of Judeo-Christian traditions by purely disengaging himself from the socio-historical conditions. This needs to be deconstructed by all means. Melancholy figuring in the early writings of Benjamin needs to be seen as the product of a tussle between the radical spirit of his youth and further the assimilative tendencies of the university education which is deeply socio political, where his Judaic sprit of enquiry juggled with the so called interpretative conditions of the modern subject. Benjamin by all means knew that only with the tradition one can encounter certain dissimilar assemblages of the present. European modernism is here getting radically redefined. As Uwe Steiner comments:

> What imbues Benjamin's early writings with a standard and at times straining pathos is to a considerable extent that gesture of absoluteness that perceives any form of concreteness as a betrayal, if not of the idea, then of its unconditionality and purity. It is not merely in the nature of things but clearly the author's intention that this pathos occasionally verges on the religious. (Steiner 2003: 23)

Developing his idea of melancholy, Benjamin diverted his intellectual paths from many of his predecessors including Freud and traversed through other ideas such as revolution, beauty, change and claims of truth. The "subject of melancholy" for Benjamin was more than a subject under a pertinent psychological analysis; on the other hand, such a subject has a certain potential to rearticulate the sense of "loss". This characteristic of the subject, needless to say, should be seen as a historical contingency that would provide new meanings to know the world. Knowing the world, hence, for Benjamin was a method of understanding *Stimmung*.

Instead of looking at the individual as an isolated phenomenon on whom melancholy can be invested, Benjamin looks at the serious internal contradictions of the society where ideas are constantly at odds, and schisms are further developing. Benjamin found the historical concept of the Weimar era as the most suitable one to revise the theological questions of history he was deeply in trouble with. In his *Theses on the Philosophy of History*, particularly in Thesis Two, he develops the argument: 'the idea of happiness is indissolubly bound up with the idea of redemption' (Benjamin 2003: 389). This is definitely an anti-Freudian idea if we look at 'redemption' far too removed from the pathological condition as Freud understood. This idea, by and large, is spread all over Benjamin's writings, and needless to say, in these early writings as well. However, a periodization of Benjamin's writings, it seems, might occlude some of the pertinent questions of melancholy as that would perhaps put some of the author's writings in one period by locating the socio- historical conditions. It is important to understand how in Benjamin the notion of melancholy is all pervasive, but with some definite ways of understanding it. Critics and theoreticians including Uwe Steiner, Ilit Ferber and many others have so far been looking at this problem by categorizing his writings with respect to definite points of time in history. While such a method cannot be completely rejected, one needs to develop another methodology to understand this all pervasive nature of melancholy in Benjamin's writings by engaging with some debates of modernity.

Benjamin challenges the question of the normative understanding of the subject as understood in the phenomenology of Edmund Husserl or in the cyclical history of Hegel. If phenomenology could arrest the sensations of the subject by positing the "intentionality", the subject for Benjamin has already derided a number of anti-intentional methods by delving deep into certain traditions from where her/his idea of knowing the world crops up. For Benjamin, the act of knowing the world is the act of submerging deep into the tradition and a recovery from there as such a recovery is necessary for a political idea, where ethics plays a crucial role. Ilit Ferber looks at this question and comments: 'Man is not sad or mournful for a specific loss relating to his subjective, contingent existence; his melancholy is linguistic, and it touches directly on his inability to execute his linguistic essence—that of naming nature' (Ferber 2003: 141). Needless to say, Ferber's intricate analysis of Benjamin's idea of melancholy partially obscures the field of "linguistic essence", which otherwise was considered as the relationship of language and the world. However, this analysis, despite its stringent stress on linguistic compatibility poses questions of the ethical dimension. Benjamin's attempt was to make the notion of melancholy a key factor of modernism, where man despite her/his need for the change would properly recognize the traditional impulse, and would try to translate the corpus of theological and mythical roots to progress. Melancholy is not an antidote against something; it is inherent in modern man as a means to articulate a new sense of progress and understanding.

Examining the works of Franz Kafka, Benjamin points out one of the rare instances that is in operation in Kafka's writings. Benjamin states that 'Oblivion is the container from which the inexhaustible, intermediate world in Kafka's stories presses toward the light' (Benjamin 1992:127). The key terms in this statement are "oblivion" and "light". It is clear from this statement that "oblivion" is a state of inertia or non-functional terrain where character, writer or the act of writing subsumes to certain pressures. Undoubtedly, the Judeo-Christian tradition which functions in the background of Kafka's writings cannot be forgotten here. It is from here that man in his journey started losing something. But unlike the situation of a modern subject we have seen before, this is not such a situation where one mourns the loss of any object. This "oblivion" is necessarily an implicated awareness that in the step toward progress, one has let loose of something—necessarily a linguistic question, where the struggle toward the *Stimmung* is predicated on a memory- less human condition. The "light" refers to Benjamin's idea of redemption. In order to progress to this "light", one needs to take away the coats of adornment and austerity. Benjamin might later connote this progress as the event of language. In a nutshell, one can surmise that the dichotomy of modernism essentially lies in this incomprehensibility: the sense of creating a new meaning to life and the essential ethico-political question of man, which is unevenly answered and understood.

Benjamin further develops this ethico-political stance by looking at the potential of messiah in Theses IX in 'Theses on the Philosophy of History'. Interpreting Paul Klee's painting "Angelus Novus", Benjamin observes the double-headed angel with one head turning toward the past and another one to the future: 'The angel would like to stay, awaken the dead, and make whole what has been smashed. But a storm is blowing from Paradise; it has got caught in his wings with such violence that the angel can no longer close them. This storm irresistibly propels him into future to which his back is turned, while the pile of debris before him grows skyward. This storm is what we call progress' (Ibid: 249). It is here the central debate of modernism emerges. On the one hand, the angel with its head turned to the future indicates the rapid progress and the act of movement—far too radically developed from the previous art movements and eras; on the other hand, this angel is pictured in such a way that in its movement it cannot clearly see the future. At the same time, the eye turned to the past never divorces itself from what remains there. This inherent contradiction is the dialectic of European modernism as the idea of progress here is not developed as fully welcoming, but with stutters on the brink of internal pulls of traditions and destructions. Though a number of historians have interpreted this passage differently, for our purpose to understand the modern subject and European melancholy, the observation by Max Pensky is essential. Pensky, situating Benjamin's *Trauerspiel*, comments that the whole oeuvre of Benjamin's studies of allegory, myth and language lies in "overcoming melancholia" (Pensky 1993: 150). Right from *The Origin of the German Tragic Drama* to *Theses on the Philosophy of History*, Benjamin never wants to shed off melancholy completely. Benjamin, contrary to what Pensky thought, was not warning of the danger of allegorical pessimism as a negative outbreak of German Tragic drama; on the other hand, he was trying to locate this as the dialectical reversal of historical conditions.

Melancholy cannot in this context be seen to draw its social authority simply from any privileged relation to the life as truth. Rather, truthful life is derived through melancholy's proximity to the rhetoric of sadness. The legacy of this sadness for the writer's intention to mark her/his writing persists in two ways: First, the sadness imports not only the theological/spiritual but also the legal constraints of truth telling and potential punishment for error into the course of its expression. Second, sadness is marked by a cultural production entwined with our notions of relationship to the "other". Melancholy turns out to be a discourse that both requires and shapes "truth" according to certain notions of theo-societal and political conditions. What Benjamin outlined needs to be seen as the pathology of the age and not as an individual malaise. More than the pathological and psychoanalytic features ascribed to melancholy, we find in Benjamin its liberation from the constraints of mental trapdoors and societal conflicts. The dichotomy of modernity, needless to say, assumes its significance when we understand the potential of melancholy far from its fixations to subjects and expositions.

Sebaldian Melancholia

In the writings of W.G. Sebald, we come across a series of issues connected to this dichotomy of modern melancholy perceived differently and constituted in divergent ways in the geographical and political map of modern Europe. Each of Sebald's texts is an enquiry into the nature of truth production by disengaging with the normative parameters of textual production and consumption. The diversified voices and the protagonists, who most of the time are nameless, constitute stuttering mechanisms of textual self determination. In each of his works, Sebald makes an enquiry into the peripatetic nature of Europe by engaging his protagonists with a number of historical and social questions. While stationed at different places and spaces in time in the context of post war Europe, his protagonists are disengaged from the act of any particular truth production—that is, coming in terms with certain particular moments or events in history to explain the condition of Europe or any significant space/place for that matter; on the other hand, their engagement with a specific space/place are extended to a phenomenal trope of other discourses making the space/place a matter of elongated narration. The issue of the "particular" in Sebald is not the derivative of any singularity connected to the subject formation, which we have seen in European modernism. Hence, Sebald's texts invite many questions concerned with the nature and function of modern melancholy.

Examining Sebald's works in the light of European melancholy and historicity, J.J. Long cites Wolf Lepenies's work *Melancholy and Society* and sums up the argument: 'Lepenies argues that the melancholy of the intellectual becomes a topos in Europe at the point when capitalism and the Protestant work ethic install the *vita activa* as the behavioural norm within the bourgeois society and marginalise the *vita contemplative* (XXI) (Long 2002: 5) Long states how Lepenies drew examples from the 18th century German bourgeoisie and the conditions of the post-war "Federal Republic's reaction to the mortal and political catastrophe of Nazism" (Ibid: 6). The given examples make Long conclude that 'Like memory, then, melancholy is an aspect of Sebald's texts that might appear to be irreducibly individual or psychological, but once historicized emerges as one more element in a wider exploration of modernity' (Ibid). The central contention here is melancholy's inseparable affinity to modernity and the deeply rooted nexus with the creation of a new language of modernity.

For the purpose of making melancholy's inextricable links with the space and place in the context of the dichotomy of European subject formation, we will concentrate on two works of Sebald (*The Rings of Saturn* and *Austerlitz*), where he evokes a new modality of melancholy far deviant from the pathological case associated with that. *The Rings of Saturn* is Sebald's most peripatetic work, a work in which the writer traverses many times and spaces, a work of multiple connotations, rhizomatic references and a number of intertextual and contra-textual ideas figure in. As the title indicates, Saturn is normally considered to be the planet of melancholy by astrologers. The rings around it are usually perceived as dimensions that mark the planet's movement. In other words, they signify a sense of outer disturbance, which may not allow the planet to possess its own integrity in the solar system. Scientifically, one knows that these rings are the formation of dust. This significant title, taken into the historical and political spectrum of Europe, offers an immense opportunity to understand the internal disturbance of the continent.

The protagonist's journey along the coastline of Lowestoft in *The Rings of Saturn* brings into focus his attachment to two different times: a time when he used to identify the life of the fishermen as part of nature and the time of the present, where the space/place has turned out to be emptied of the vast richness of nature. Sebald's protagonist memorizes one such instance: 'As I tried to suppress the mounting sense of dizziness, breathing out and taking a step backwards, I thought I saw something of an odd, pallid colour move on the shoreline. I crouched down and, overcome by a sudden panic, looked over the edge. A couple lay down there, in the bottom of the pit, I thought: a man stretched full length over another body of which nothing was visible but the legs, spread and angled. In the startled moment, when that image went through me, which lasted an eternity, it seemed as the man's feet twitched like those of one just hanged. Now, though, he lay still, and the woman too was still and motionless. Misshapen, like some great mollusc washed ashore, they lay there, to all appearances a single being, a many limbed, two-headed monster that had drifted in from far out at sea, the last of the prodigious species, its life ebbing from it with each breath expired through its nostrils' (Sebald 2002: 68). This description of the long dead and gone creature and the perverse comparison with the human bodies signifies the destruction of nature brought out by the humans and the disappointing state of visuality. What the protagonist tried to see is not there at all. But the couple and their movements, needless to say, signify some sense of an impending destruction quite akin to the nameless creature the protagonist tries to imagine. The act of mourning here is performed through visuality. Sebald's protagonist constantly narrates whatever comes before his areas of vision. The protagonist is not mourning about a fixed loss, but a context where elements of history are hidden and need to be recovered.

In the narrative part IV of *The Rings of Saturn*, Sebald's protagonist internalizes melancholy by journeying through the troubled life of the patron saint, who 'was the son of a king from Dacia or Denmark, who married a French princess in Paris' (Ibid: 86). We read further: 'During the wedding night, the story goes, he was afflicted with a sense of profound unworthiness. Today, he is supposed to have said to his bride, our bodies are adorned, but tomorrow they will be food for worms. Before the break of day, he fled, making a pilgrimage to Italy, where he lived in solitude until he felt the power to work miracles arising within him' (Ibid). This internalization leads the protagonist to confess, 'This story of the burning of the frozen substance of lice has, of late, meant much to me, and I wonder now whether inner coldness and desolation may not be the pre-condition for making the world believe, by a kind of fraudulent showmanship, that one's own wretched heart is still aglow' (Ibid). This strategy of Sebald can be termed as "declassifying the self" as the protagonist here is not fully conscious of his own state, but internalizes the melancholy nature of the space/place by getting into the story of the patron saint. The space/place of the patron saint create a different *topos* for the protagonist as this space/place is historically brought into his mind to create a melancholy of the present. In another narrative VII from the same text, we find an extension of this when the protagonist goes to see the poet Michael Hamburger. In his meeting with Hamburger, unlike what we have seen in the previous instance, we find the protagonist deeply involved in the second person narrative to create a sense of melancholy. Sebald writes: 'We talked about the deserted, soundless months of August. For weeks, said Michael, there is not a bird to be seen. It is as if everything was somehow hollowed out. Everything is on the point of decline, and only the weeds flourish: bindweed strangles the shrubs, the yellow roots of nettles creep onward in the soil, burdock stands a whole head taller than oneself, brown rot and greenfly are everywhere, and even the sheets of paper on which one endeavours to put together a few words and sentences seem covered in mildew' (Ibid: 181). In this description also we assimilate a sense of loss and loneliness essentially the one brought in tandem with the space/place where the poet lives. However, such a description does not give us a standard sense of the "loss of an object", on the other hand, it situates a subject under construction in peculiar circumstance of redefining the space/place. Sebald's preoccupation with space/place more than its historic reference is seriously predicated on the need of reconstructing the past in a situation of ruin and decay. Furthermore, this signifies a gesture of identifying with the "other" to grapple with the sense of modern melancholy.

The innumerable references to various aspects of nature and natural calamities have added a special dimension to Sebald's melancholy in *The Rings of Saturn*. The peripatetic feature of the text distills fixed notions of time and space. Most of the protagonists in this text are forced to construct melancholy out of their visuality and historical awareness. Whether Sebald understood history as melancholy is still a question worth debating. This special feature of Sebald further accentuates into the act of writing by the protagonist as we come across another protagonist in his walks through Orford mourns: 'And today I do not raise my eyes from my work. I have become almost invisible, to some extent like a dead man. Perhaps that is why it appears to me that this world which I have very nearly left behind is shrouded in some peculiar mystery' (Ibid: 255). Unlike a Freudian subject, Sebald's protagonist never wishes to be part of one peculiar loss of any object. The various strands his narratives are woven indicate the essential philosophic question of modern melancholy—the one created out of abject rejection of a particular subject/object relationship and one to one correspondence.

Sebald invokes Benjamin's Theses in *On the Natural History of Destruction*. Studying closely Alexander Kluge's works on war, Sebald tries to highlight the after effects of the aerial warfare on Dresden. The picture that Sebald draws is indeed dismal and grey. Moreover, this picture gels well with the idea of ruin and decay, the twin favourite themes of the writer. Born after the Holocaust, it is all the more natural that Sebald had in him the pangs of agony and guilt consciousness. Extending his tropes of vision, Sebald claims that 'The silence above the ruins is striking. It seems as if nothing is going on, but appearances are deceptive insofar as fires are still burning in the cellars, moving underground from one coal hole to another. Many crawling creatures. Some parts of the city stink. There are groups out looking for corpses' (Sebald 2003: 67). The description of such a gory detail entails a withdrawal from the European city as well as a submission to this war torn scenario. What is striking here is Sebald's citation of Benjamin's angel, the messianic power, which it is believed would redeem this crisis—a crisis of destruction. Though Sebald's ends his powerful essay by the citation of Benjamin, he no longer seems to extend his argument in relation to melancholy. David Kauffmann states that 'the identification with the angels is intimately linked with Sebald's predilection for panoramas and maps. His narrators like an aerial view. This allows them to spatialize time (a Benjaminian trick) and see in the landscape the traces of the depredations of history in a flash' (Kauffmann 2008: 117).

The most widely discussed and his last published text *Austerlitz* complicates the sense of melancholy beyond spatial configurations. May be it is in this text, one can say that Sebald reverts all modalities of seeing, perceiving and reconfiguring. *Austerlitz* is a text of constant mourning—far beyond Freudian and a later Lacanian idea connecting *a la* subject—but one which urges the reader to find its expressions elsewhere. Among the various themes involved in this text including the search for Austerlitz's parents, the second person narrator's destabilizing accounts and the vast panorama of architectures and ruins, the text problematizes the relative notion of space and time. Though we are aware from where Austerlitz begins his journey, the later peripatetic and confusing space/place configuration of the text irreversibly constructs a mental space of an irrevocable loss. Sebald tries to highlight this loss at a macro level by situating Austerlitz's enquiries.

Austerlitz talks about the vision of his friend and his opinion earlier in the text: 'As Alphonso has told him, said Austerlitz, there is really no reason to suppose that lesser beings are devoid of sentient life. We are not alone in dreaming at night for, quite apart from dogs and other domestic creatures whose emotions have been bound with ours for many thousands of years, the smaller mammals such as mice and moles also live in a world that exists only in their minds while they are asleep, as we can detect from their eye movements, and who knows, said Austerlitz, perhaps moths dream as well, perhaps a lettuce in the garden dreams at it looks up at the moon by night' (Sebald 2001: 94). This passage, above all, is a testament to the fact that how a boy in disillusionment can find solace with the animal world. But interestingly, one never finds a great pleasure in this identification or realization of what happens in the animal world. This sense of observation is coming out of deep melancholy, which turns the mind of the narrator to Austerlitz's private realm of understanding. Again we find Sebald trying to evoke the sense of melancholy from the narrative of the other. Melancholy here is not an individuated potential that is deeply interiorized; rather, it is something spread from individual to individual, and understood as a communicative strategy.

Later, we find Austerlitz in the narration of the protagonist getting melancholic in the streets of Terezen, where loneliness and abandonment haunt him. Sebald writes: '..... I met no one all morning in the straight, deserted streets of Terezin, except for a mentally disturbed man who crossed my path among the lime tres of the park with the fountain, telling I have no idea what tale in a kind of broken German while frantically waving his arms, before he too, still clutching the hundred-crown note I had given him, seemed to be swallowed up by the earth, as they say, even as he was running off. ...... I could not imagine, said Austerlitz, who might inhabit these desolate buildings, or if anyone lived there at all, although on the other hand I had noticed that long rows of dustbins with large numbers on them in red paint were ranged against the walls of the backyards' (Ibid: 189-190). The narrative interspersed with the photographs of places accentuates further the melancholy. Austerlitz's narrative is partly his own and partly that of his narrator/protagonist. Many times we find the mood of melancholy swinging between the two and the text becoming a cornucopia of disturbed memories, narrations and the photographs. Austerliz's search is based on the dichotomy of European melancholy, that is, can history be a significant element to understand where we come from and where are we going? When history's genuine duty—that is, to narrate objectively what happened fails and the consequent narratives are mired in doubts and confusions, Sebald seems to suggest that the protocols of memory get entangled with deep sense of melancholy. It is difficult at this juncture to claim that Sebald is using this melancholy nature of these protagonists with respect to different space/place articulations as a positive aspect. From these disturbing senses of wanderings and peripatetic configuration of narratives deep inside Europe, particularly in the post- Holocaust scenario, one never can rework the past without getting into a tangled web of melancholy. Europe is the site of endless difference and discriminations. Hence, the normative methodology of understanding history, melancholy and memory radically differs.

Since all Sebald's texts contain a number of photographs that constantly refer to and switch off to various situations both in and outside the text, it is important to look at the relationship of the text and photographs keeping in mind the idea of melancholy. Sebald seems to operate at a non-discursive level of engaging with the reader. As the rings of Saturn are meant to produce a deep sense of inwardness, the inward looking subject of Sebald, unlike in other modernist writers such as Gunter Grass, Herta Mueller, Jerzy Kosinsky, or with Thomas Mann, tries to make this "inward looking" habit projected outside so that at every moment of the walks of the protagonists, they constantly rearticulate the space/ place of their seeing. At times, one can surmise that the narrative seems to teeter at the brink of some sense of unbelievable domain, and it is in this sense, the photographs work the question of the intended. The desolate doorsteps, corridors of the Terezin barracks are all visually more powerful than the recounted accounts of Austerlitz. The sense of wonder attested to the architecture and the closeted idea of the ruins become more melancholy evoking in the photographs. In other words, Sebald might have intended to offer a new grammar of European melancholy by such interspersed photographs in his texts.

Looking at the interrelationship between photographs and melancholy, J.J. Long writes: 'as a technical mode of representation that allows for potentially infinite mechanical reproduction..... embodies the principles of technological rationality and seriality that govern capitalist production' (Long 2007: 5). This finds true when we understand the complicated issue of narration as sometimes a failure to address the issues. Narration per se may not be sufficient to bring into focus certain questions of history and the associated ideas of melancholy. Nina Plikan Straus also addresses this issue in 'Sebald, Wittgenstein, and the Ethics of Memory' by stating that 'Sebald's exhibition of the eighty-one photos 'entrusted' to the narrator by Austerlitz becomes a mnemonic device aimed at triggering buried connections that unlock parts of Holocaust history' (Strauss 2009: 51). In *Austerlitz*, it can be seen that this mnemonic device is used to produce time to time melancholy, which counters the static notion of time and space or the deviant ideas of the same perceived in modernity. Sebald, thus, tries to offer us a new perspective of time/space by making his texts deeply melancholic by situating history and memory incriminating each other and interrogating the past in various ways.

The (Un)quenchable Taste of Language

In light of the above observations, we find melancholy in European modernism is a much challenging and complicated discourse. It has several strands associated with theological, political, historical and philosophical questions from time to time. Any uniform way of looking at melancholy will never give justice to the wider philosophic and aesthetic dimensions associated with it. Melancholia becomes a condition to perceive the differences that shaped modernity in Europe. The only ethical and political idea adduced to it in Benjamin's writing, hence may, suffice us with other possibilities of noticing the unnoticeable space/place of European modernity. Given the fact that European modernity is an uneven phenomenon, one needs to engage in specific caveats of thought to untangle its deeper notions of historical and political circumstances. As Jonathan Flatley says, 'Walter Benjamin saw melancholia as a definitely historical problem related to the experience of modernity. In his view melancholia is no longer a personal problem requiring cure or catharsis, but is evidence of historicity of one's subjectivity, indeed the very substance of that historicity' (Flatley 2008: 3). This perhaps may be the juncture where melancholy assumes the notion of the ethical and political. The affective conditions of this ethico-political question so far derided in the study of modernism finds their expression in Benjamin's writings.

To map this affective condition of melancholy, one definitely has to re-imagine the "loss". There are ways of doing this and one such way is the fictional intervention into history, where as Sebald has done, the space/place of the subject becomes tangential to the claims of any particular claims of truth. The central dichotomy of European modernism is thrust on paranoia of reclaiming the "loss" pertaining to melancholy. Sebald's texts have opened up an opportunity that one can reclaim and re- imagine the "loss" to constitute a new subject position—both historically and politically viable in contemporary times. Sebald's melancholy resists against all existing theoretical formulations of the same and reconstitutes a system of differences, perhaps the most wanted and needed ones, in a Benjaminian sense, where melancholy assumes a sense of positivity countering *a*historical postulations and theological dimensions.

The unevenly perceived European modernity has a lot to offer to melancholy. The subject of melancholy transforms the parameters of language, system of thoughts and progresses as Benjamin outlined to the sphere of an ethical positioning, which is indeed the index of European philosophical thought. The debate on language, at all its outlandish situations, is centered on this idea of perpetual difference of space/place. As observed by William S. Allen, '...the transformation of melancholy arises when between the muteness of its need to speak and the muteness of its endless lament, alongside or parallel to the singularity of the cadaver, the only true mark of finitude, whose company writing seeks so as to find its own ambivalence' (Allen 2008: 1085). However, this question of language sandwiched between the lament and speech, is what is at the center of Benjamin's anxiety, which is later transgressed by the writing of W.G. Sebald. This is where a positivistic idea of melancholy is created and a progression to understand the subject is oriented.

References

Allen, William S., 'Melancholy and Parapraxis: Rewriting History in Benjamin and Kafka', *MLN.* 122:5 (2008): 1068-1087.

Benjamin, Walter, *Illuminations*, trans. Harry Zohn (London: Fontana Press, 1992).

Benjamin, Walter, *Selected Writings*, Vol. 4, eds. Howard Eiland and Michael Jennings (Cambridge Mass: Harvard University Press, 2003).

Ferber, Ilit, *Philosophy and Melancholy: Benjamin's Early Reflections on Theater and Language* (Stanford: Stanford University Press, 2013).

Flatley, Jonathan, *Affective Mapping: Melancholia and the Politics of Modernism* (Cambridge: Harvard University Press, 2008).

Freud, Sigmund, 'Mourning and Melancholia', *The Standard Edition of the Complete Psychological Works of Sigmund Freud*. Vol. 14, trans. James Strachey (London: Hogarth Press, 1986).

Green, Andre, *On Private Madness* (Madison, Conn: International Univerisities Press, 1986).

Kauffman, David, 'Angels Visit the Sense of Disgrace: Melancholy and Trauma from Sebald, Benjamin and Back' in *Cultural Critique* 70(2008): 94-119.

Kristeva, Julia, *Black Sun*, trans. Leon S. Roudiez (New York: Columbia University Press, 1992).

Long, J.J., *W.G. Sebald-Image, Archive, Modernity* (New York: Columbia University Press, 2007).

Pensky, Max, *Melancholy Dialectics* (Amherst: University of Massachussetts Press, 1993).

Sebald, W.G., *Austerlitz*, trans. Anthea Bell (New York: The Modern Library, 2001).

Sebald, W.G., *On the Natural History of Destruction*, trans. Anthea Bell (New York: Random House, 2003).

Sebald, W.G., *The Rings of Saturn*, trans. Michael Hulse (London: Vintage, 2002).

Steiner, Uwe, *Walter Benjamin: An Introduction to His Work and Thought*, trans. Michael Winkler (Chicago and London: The University of Chicago Press, 2010).

Straus, Nina Palkan, 'Sebald, Wittgenstein and the Ethics of Memory'. *Comparative Literature*. 61.1. (2009): 43-53.

Melancholy and the World
The Genesis of a Modern Concept

Soumick Dey

> *Woyzeck: it makes me shudder when I think that the Earth turns itself about in a single day! What a waste of time. Where will it all end? I can't even look at a mill wheel any more without becoming melancholy.*
>
> Georg Buchner, *Woyzeck* (1963: 109)

The Problem of World Destroying Tiredness

In the preface to her edited volume *The Nature of Melancholy: From Aristotle to Kristeva* (Radden 2000), Jennifer Radden laments the contemporary disinterest with this idea which dominated European cultural history for more than two millennia. Compiled at the threshold of the 21st century the book claims to pay 'homage to its past' (Ibid: vii). It is then not without a certain sense of irony that more than fifteen years later Byung-Chul Han, a Korean-German philosopher and cultural theorist would categorise the so-called post-modern, neo-liberal society of the West as a 'burnout society' (Han 2015) suffering from a kind of 'world destroying' (Ibid: 28; Handke 1994) depression and tiredness. Rather provocatively Byung diagnoses this experience of exhaustion or tiredness as an effect of our inability to think of any radical "Other". Consequently our contemporary "Self" is thrown into the violent excess of a degrading and corrupt immanence. According to Byung, it is as a result of this vanishing of the notion of any transcendental "Other", in our current 'achievement society', that we are hurling *ourselves* towards an 'inferno of the same' (Han 2017: 1) which cannot sustain any radical negativity but merely the positivity of consumable differences[1]. Moreover this pull towards the "same" has become identical with a narcissistic withdrawal from reality into the self which has become invested with the maximum of libido, making it impossible to distinguish between the "self" and the "other". In other words, the world has become only so many variations of the self. Hence depression is no longer merely a pathological disorder of the subject but an objective and dominant affliction of our contemporary social reality. Han writes:

> Depression is a narcissistic malady. It derives from overwrought, pathologically distorted self-reference. The narcissistic-depressive subject has exhausted itself and worn itself down. Without a world to inhabit, it has been abandoned by the Other...Today's narcissistic "achievement-subject" seeks out success above all. Finding success validates the One through the Other. Thereby, the Other is robbed of otherness and degrades into a mirror of the One—a mirror affirming the latter's image. This logic of recognition ensnares the narcissistic achievement-subject more deeply in the ego. The corollary is success-induced depression. (Ibid: 3)

The "work" of such 'narcissistic- melancholy'[2] in a world 'abandoned by the other', where all that remains is the continuous and narcissistic consumption of differences, seems threateningly identical with a pathological form of overwhelming self-absorption. Our current experience of melancholy as a result of this surplus of positivity, however, does not allow us to miss the following irony: Freud's 1915 essay 'Mourning and Melancholy' (Freud 1959), one of the last genuine theories of melancholy, paradoxically views melancholic narcissism as different from other types of narcissism, categorising it essentially as an 'impoverishment of the ego on a grand scale' (Ibid: 155). We shall come back to this point in detail later on in the essay. Be that as it may, the response to our first contradiction—between a determined disinterest and a growing experience of melancholy—seems to be self-evident. Precisely a surplus of our subjective experience of melancholy seems to prevent us from treating it as an object of thought. A separation between our quasi-aesthetic and worldly experience of melancholy and a clear concept of melancholy is impossible without a certain dialectic mode of thinking which re-articulates the value of negativity while thinking through this problem.

It would be the primary contention of this paper that when Freud wrote his 'Mourning and Melancholia' he was keenly aware of this dialectical spirit which was at work behind his theorization of *both* mourning and melancholia, albeit they unfold in two different fashions. While the work of mourning provides for a dialectical resolution to the problem of loss by detaching the self from the object in the world—and thereby allowing a certain symbolic resolution to the crisis—the work of melancholy operates through preserving the loss *itself* as an "object" without any symbolic closure. What we find in melancholy is nothing less than a dialectic of the Subject and Other which is never resolved but always kept alive like an open wound. This is the negative operation at work in Freud's concept of melancholy which we would like to explore further. Our task, therefore, is to *distinguish* between a concept of melancholy sustained by negativity, and its contemporary experience as surplus positivity. In order to do so, we propose a genealogical study of the concept to argue that this element of negativity, and its relation to melancholy is quintessentially *modern*: it appears as a consequence of a shift in the notion of melancholy that came about during the Renaissance. However in order to understand this shift we need to first highlight the nature of the problem during the Middle Ages.

The Analogical Mode of Thinking

The Medieval Problem of *Accidie*

A major factor governing the theory of *accidie*[3] in early medieval scholarship, particularly in the writings of the patristic tradition, was to associate this "pathological" condition exclusively with the lives of the monks. Such 'monastic melancholy'[4] was identified through a constellation of psychological symptoms ranging from *desperation*— the self-destructive complacency resulting from a feeling of futility of spiritual life because of the certainty of being always already condemned—to *curiousitas* which signifies the insatiable and distracting desire of seeing for the pleasure of seeing itself.[5] It is, however, in the last decade of the 4th century in Cassian's documentation of the lives of those desert fathers of the cenobitic tradition (desert fathers who were most susceptible to this malady) that we find some of the most extraordinarily insightful psychological description of the "noonday demon".[6] He writes of *accidie*:

> And when this has taken possession of some unhappy soul, it produces dislike of the place, disgust with the cell, and disdain and contempt of the brethren... it also makes the man lazy and sluggish about all manner of work which has to be done within the enclosure of his dormitory. It does not suffer him to stay in his cell, or to take any pains about reading and he groans because he can do no good while he stays there....he cries up distant monasteries and those which are a long way off and describes such places as more profitable and better suited for salvation.... Lastly he fancies that he will never be well while he stays in that place, unless he leaves his cell (in which he is sure to die if he stops in it any longer) and takes himself off from thence as quickly as possible. (Cassian in Radden 2000: 71-72)

Clearly one cannot miss the ambiguity that glaringly stands out in this description of *accidie* as the medieval idea of "sloth". Even modern critics, who analyze the works of Freud, often make a similar mistake of neatly categorizing melancholy as passivity as against mourning as work. Cassian, however, paints a different picture of the sluggish man whose passivity is not all the time physiological in nature. It is in fact an inactivity of the soul. Cassian comments that all the inadequacies of the disease of *accidie* can be summed up in the single verse of David 'where he says "My soul slept from weariness", that is from accidie. Quite rightly does he say, not that his body, but that his soul slept' (Ibid: 73). However, this slumber of the soul is not always expressed by the passivity of the body or behaviour. In fact, the passivity of the soul can be *dissimulated* as restlessness or distraction when the individual experiences an active urge to flee his cell, and proclaim that the enjoyment of salvation lies elsewhere, in some distant monastery. *Accidie*, then, produces a deserter, a runaway who displays the risk of getting entangled in secular business. It is important to emphasise this point. The slumber of the soul can lead to physical sloth, but it can also mask itself as an active force which detracts the subject from his righteous path of a *vita contemplativa*; or, better, the contemplative life which comprises a vertical and ascendant movement from the natural to the supernatural is not only interrupted by *accidie* which blocks this path of ascendency, but it produces a counter-force which hurls the subject back into the corrupt world of 'secular business'. *Accidie* in its essence is, therefore, a force which not only blocks the path of a true Christian life of contemplation but creates a counter-force which throws him back into the world. This is its first and fundamental characteristic. Moreover, the malady is deceptive in character often dissimulating itself as a virtue. This is its second characteristic feature. Hence Cassian writes:

> Then the disease suggests that he ought to show courteous and friendly hospitalities to the brethren, and pay visits to the sick, whether near at hand or far off. He talks too about some dutiful and religious offices. That it would be a real work of piety to go more frequently to visit that religious woman, devoted to the service of god, who is deprived of all support of kindred... and that he ought piously to devote his time to these things instead of staying uselessly and with no profit in his cell. (Ibid: 72)

Following Evagrius Ponticus—who was one of the earliest church fathers to propose a systematic study of the eight vices which were later transformed into the seven cardinal sins by Pope Gregory in the late 6th century—Cassian viewed *accidie* as caused by the Devil. And, like most other temptations, it was masked as a virtue because it is in the Devil's nature to dissimulate. Therefore, the cure for *accidie* was to first identify the true nature of one's actions. But in order to identify *accidie* as what it truly is, one had to perform an act of self-examination. However, self-analysis is already part of a *vita contemplative* because it brings the self back to itself (a withdrawal from the world and return to the self) to continue its upward journey, but this time scaling over the wall that *accidie* has erected in the first place. Therefore, the cure of *accidie,* or, at least the first and most important step was to recognize the disease in its true nature which would give the person the incentive to stay and fight. To give into the disease is to give into its deception which induces a state of flight from the true object of desire of the Christian subject: the divine truth. So Cassian writes: 'For more frequently and more severely will the enemy attack one who.... look for safety neither in victory nor in fighting but in flight' (Ibid: 73).

Though it is tempting to believe Agamben when he argues that there is already a dialectic of desire at work in patristic understanding of *accidie,* his argument becomes contentious precisely at this point. Agamben maintains that 'what afflicts the slothful is not, therefore, the awareness of an evil, but on the contrary, the contemplation of the greatest good. *Acedie* is precisely the vertiginous and frightened withdrawal (*recessus*) when faced with the task implied by the place of man before God" (Agamben 1993: 6). This analysis, in my view, is a too early diagnosis of a dialectical understanding of melancholy which unfolds around the quattrocento. It seems to me that for the patristic tradition, and specially in Cassian,[7] *accidie* was essentially treated as an obstruction to a contemplative religious life—a *vita contemplativa*—characterized by a hierarchical mode of thinking based on, what Jacob Taubes identifies as, the *analogical* style of medieval theological meditations.[8] Agamben argues that for the patristic tradition and even later *accidie* embodied a logic where the object of desire is identified and recognized as the divine truth, but the path to the fulfillment of such desire is obstructed, such that the loss of the object of desire (withdrawal from divine good) is dialectically placed with the maintenance of the knowledge of the desired object. We, on the other hand, have tried to show that *accidie* induced, precisely, a kind of false knowledge which not only blocked his access to the truly desired divine knowledge but feigned to offer him satisfaction (thereby deviating him from his true calling), a life devoted to the pursuit of divine truth. *Accidie,* like most of the other temptations, signified a kind of immediate enjoyment which threatened the very existence of a single and final enjoyment in the divine truth. In that sense it might be argued that it functioned, from a psychoanalytic perspective, like the 'Id/It' as against the Christian 'Ego', the latter sustaining the desire for the divine truth. The temptations were objective and material moments within which the subject found little zones of fulfillment while a more profound enjoyment and divine fulfillment eluded her. It is this autonomy of enjoyment (Id) as against the final and ultimate fulfillment of the Ego (which threatened to cut itself off from the 'body' of the Christian Subject (here 'body' of the Christian subject has to be taken as identical with the 'body' of the church). There is something essentially comic—in so far as comedy is about finding supplementary and momentary enjoyments "elsewhere" rather than clinging onto unfulfilled desire—about this idea of melancholy as *accidie* in medieval thinking (Zupancic 2008: 62-71). It is this autonomous enjoyment that the Church fathers were quick to attack, identifying it as a "blockage". Blockage did not simply imply that the subject is prevented from attaining the final object of desire in spite of the knowledge of its presence. Rather, it implied the production of false knowledge which offered a new path leading to some other autonomous fulfillment elsewhere. We have to make this crucial distinction between the medieval understanding of melancholy and its relation to *vita contemplativa* where it functions as a kind of 'comic-materialist' obstruction,[9] and its Renaissance counterpart. In Renaissance, as we would try to argue in the next section, melancholy functions as a kind of unavoidable "tragic" effect or by-product of intellectual life—a *vita speculativa*—governed by a dialectical mode of thinking.

The problem of melancholy as a type of blockage rather than a simple withdrawal (which is merely its symptom) can be identified in Chrysostom's exhortation to his protégé Stagirius. Written around 380-381, this epistle describes of a condition of despondency which falls within the family of *filiae acediae* (daughters of sloth). Interestingly Stagirius' symptoms—terrifying nightmares, torment of the soul and specially despair originating from the certainty of being already condemned, and, therefore, sinking into one's own destruction expressed through an irresistible urge to commit suicide—were exclusively related to his monastic life. Therefore, Chrysostom held out to him as consolation an appeal to God's providence. It is part of God's providence that he allows the devil to tempt mankind so that Man can learn through self–defense the righteous path of the virtuous. Because God deems Stagirius strong because he has adopted the life of religion, and thereby stepping out of the audience onto the arena, he has given him this difficult task of overcoming his affliction. It is God who has provoked the devil to tempt him with this affliction so that Stagirius can be tested for his virtue: 'This despondency in turn could be overcome by the thought that it was one of those sufferings inflicted on men not by their own guilt but by divine providence' (Klibansky et al 1979: 67). This shift in the treatment of *accidie* (or despondency)—from sin to virtue, from the work of the devil to that of God—not only reflects the complex mirroring of one in the other. It indicates a further structural similarity. The treatment of despondency depends upon knowledge that in the final analysis it is nothing but a test. It is a trial which the religious man has to pass through, which necessitates a *recognition* of the divine providence as the true cause of such despondency. It is, therefore, a task—a blockage in some sense—which is set according to the spiritual strength of the athlete. Such knowledge can only provide consolation, and prepare the subject to overcome her condition. A life of contemplation devoted to the understanding, or at least the desire to decipher the symptoms of divine providence, is implicit in Chrysostom's idea of despondency.

It is very important to note here that the idea of *vita contemplativa* in the Middle Ages was identical to *contemplation Dei*. Like liturgy was a public service performed on the basis of a sovereign and divine sign, so was *vita contemplativa*, the individual service ordained by Him. And like the liturgy of the Mass in medieval Christianity was not merely a metaphorical affair but presupposed 'charismatic union between heaven and earth' (Taubes 2009: 169), so was *vita contemplativa* a *process* which imitated the cosmic and divine hierarchy through its upward journey from the affairs of the body into the affairs of the soul till one reaches the heights of divine truth. We see this operation systematically mapped out, for example in Augustinian concept of memory and its function in a life of divine contemplation. It is perhaps inevitable to associate the form of such a contemplative life with what Jacob Taubes calls analogical style of medieval thought. Taubes ingeniously argues that it is a Ptolemaic cosmological understanding which becomes the basis of the medieval theological principle of thinking known as *analogia entis.* Such analogical mode of thinking based upon a correlation between heaven and earth supports the thesis that melancholy functions as a blockage which prevents the soul to move upwards, from the mundane reality of down below to the celestial reality of the divine truth. Therefore, the only consolation of such spiritual affliction would be constant vigilance by the subject. This would allow him to recognize *accidie* as what it truly is: a temptation which is either a sin or which is part of divine providence. In fact, the consolation of a constant vigilance as a remedy against *accidie* is only possible because it has no stake in the total history of mankind. To put it simply, consolation for *accidie* was possible because *vita contemplativa,* which corresponded to a withdrawal into the self and its gradual ascension, was supported by an external cosmological hierarchy of the universe (Ptolemaic). This consolation came as a kind of vigilant contemplation where one becomes aware of the nature and origin of her thoughts and behaviors. It is a mode of thinking which is equivalent to a kind of vision which could penetrate through the obstruction which was blocking it and arrive at the transparency of the divine truth. However, this consolation which comes as vigilance against *accedie* is never objective in nature. It is purely subjective, in so far as it is personal advice given to members of the monastic order who suffer from this particular affliction. The medieval idea of accidie, and its remedy, has no historical stake in so far as it belongs exclusively to the subjective realm of the Christian individual as a 'material blockage' which might hinder the destiny of the soul at the end of its earthly journey.

Melancholy and Original Sin

It is, however, in the mystical writings of Hildegard of Bingen, that the problem of melancholy becomes a world-historical problem. In her *Causae et curae* Hildgard on one hand describes with absolute clinical precision the material symptoms of melancholy and the physical quality of the melancholy humor (black bile) while offering an absolutely fascinating world-historical explanation for its origin. As Hildegard of Bingen says, this black, bitter element, 'which releases every evil', was once a glorious and sparkling substance like crystal 'which bore the taste of good work' and 'contained in itself the wisdom and perfection of good work' (quoted by Klibansky et al 1979: 80). But when Adam decided to disobey the divine law by eating the apple, melancholy 'curdled in his blood'. Hildegard writes:

> But when Adam broke the law, the sparkle of innocence was dulled in him, and his eyes, which had formerly beheld heaven, were blinded, and his gall was changed to bitterness and his melancholy to blackness. (Ibid)

This is not simply a beautiful and visceral description of the melancholy humor but a testimony to the world-historical blindness which the Fall of Man now condemns him to. Here melancholy is truly a tragic state that afflictes the entire human history because of the original sin. It is no longer a subjective affair but has to be borne by the whole race because it indicates an original separation of the profane order from that of the sacred. It is Adam's vision which is now blinded forever so that he can no longer "naturally" behold the heavens. There can no longer be any *perception* of the heavens because it is no longer co-relative to the earth. The tragic blindness induced by the fall is also the reason for the melancholy humor to emerge and transmit through blood. This is a testimony of man being condemned to his own history here on earth with the loss of the heavens. It is, as if, the birth of world-history coincides with this loss causing the world to withdraw into itself because it is now separated from the heaven. The sickness of melancholy is also a sickness of the world. They can both be managed in order to reduce their intensity but cannot be cured. Though clearly in her understanding of the melancholic condition Hildegard drew from the ancient humorological tradition, she *anticipates* the modern understanding of melancholy as an impoverishment. Though she argues that melancholy is immediately caused by the imbalance of the humors according to the teachings of this ancient tradition, yet this improper organization of the humors is only an effect of the originary transformation of the "crystal" of wisdom and work into gall: this is distinct from the ancient tradition where we find the imbalance of the humors as the fundamental cause of melancholy. Hildegard's idea of melancholy as a world historical affliction relates melancholy to the constitutive impoverishment of the world when it is left to itself. In other words, the age of melancholy coincides with the moment when human history withdraws into itself (in order to begin) without the support of the heavens. Melancholy is, therefore, no longer a blockage to the individual salvation of the soul but a constitutive factor of the very existence of world-history which will be overcome only on the Day of Judgment. It is because of this that, unlike the problem of *accidie* in the patristic tradition, this world-historical affliction of melancholy is ultimately inconsolable. Its only cure is the transformation of a world- historical order of mankind. It is this eschatological understanding of melancholy which induces her to provide a "material" medical condition of the End of Days when the "profane" order will be overturned and the "sacred" order begins. According to Hildegard, if one of the four humors increases in a person, he becomes weak and sick, while the increase of two humors at the same time becomes unendurable. The improper rise of three humors would eventually kill the person. However, if all the four humors rise together, it would kill the person *instantaneously*. This last possibility would be actualized on that fateful day when 'all things will be smashed on the Last Day as the four elements fight among themselves' (in Radden 2000: 83). Though *accidie* was taken as a pathological disorder, its moral and theological explanation in the patristic tradition never included a radical negativity of this magnitude. It was treated more as a blockage to an analogical mode of thinking, effectuating an interruption in its hierarchic process of ascent. Only with Hildegard's do we find a concept of melancholy as a world-historical affliction which *anticipates* a thinking of the "Other" as radically negative whose trace the experience of melancholy bears. It is, however, in the intellectual environment of, what is famously called, quattrocento, particularly in Italy, that we find this problem of melancholy taking its most complicated and perhaps also its most modern shape.

Dialectical Mode of Thinking

Poetic Melancholy

When we propose that the glorification of melancholy as a positive intellectual force unfolded in the backdrop of Florentine Neo-Platonism, around the 15th century, we have to make a crucial distinction. This glorification of the intellectual implications of melancholy—what is famously called *melancholia generosa*—has to be distinguished from the notion of "poetic melancholy" which developed as a *subjective mood* in late medieval poetry and continued with varied intensity till the 19th century. It is beyond the scope of this paper to engage in detail with this transformation and its aesthetic consequences. However, it would not be irrelevant to point out one important detail which not only marks the fundamental logic of this idea of poetic melancholy but provides a point of concurrence between the two positive variations of melancholy—intellectual and aesthetic. This usage of melancholy which generally refers to the temporary mental state of a person (which can then be *transferred* on to the object that might be responsible for the generation of this mood) came to be recognized less and less as a pathological condition or even as a temperament. The transformation of the meaning of melancholy from a quality into a "mood" coincided with a certain attempt to capture this "affect" aesthetically. Hence we find the personification of *dame* mé *rencoyle* in the 15th century treatise like that of Maistre Alain Chartier, or the romance of King Rene of Anjou. Similar to the personification of *Tristesse* in *Roman de la Rose*, these late medieval portrayals of melancholy as the despairing woman of terrifying aspect, with leaden and earthy complexion, downward regard, drooping lips and halting speech, not only gave an imaginary body to an affect—a subjective mood—but informed it with humoral-pathological characteristics. This concrete aesthetic representation of melancholy was, however, recompensed by a metaphysical abstraction whose essence was simultaneously expressed in the figure of melancholy with utmost vividness. This is the idea of melancholy, not as prophetic ecstasy or brooding meditation but as heightened self-awareness. It is epitomized later by the Miltonic figure of the *Penseroso*, and even later by the salon paintings in the age of Diderot. This "poetic" mood revels in a state of complete self-absorption which ushers in the modern notion of melancholy and its poetic significance. In their ground-breaking work on the genealogy of the concept of melancholy leading to the Durer engraving of 1514, Klibansky-Panofsky-Saxl describes this subjective mood with the utmost precision.

What emerges here is the specifically "poetic" melancholy mood of the modern; a double edged feeling constantly providing its own nourishment in which the soul enjoys its own loneliness, but by this very pleasure becomes again more conscious of its solitude, the joy in grief, "the mournful joy", or "the sad luxury of woe", to use the words of Milton's successors. This modern melancholy mood is essentially an enhanced self awareness, since the ego is the pivot around which the sphere of joy and grief revolves (Klibansky et al 1979: 231).

Clearly we witness here in this notion of intensified self-consciousness a dialectic of consciousness which in the very act of accessing the knowledge about itself also gains the knowledge of its own finitude. As a subjective poetic mood, melancholy not only absorbed all its previous signification of unhappy love, sickness, death and despair, but brought about a perfect synthesis of "*Tristesse*" and "*Melancholie*", thereby producing a state of self awareness which was co-relative to the awareness of death. This "tragic" understanding of melancholy is, therefore, intricately entwined with a certain mode of intellectual thinking informed by a deep sense of negativity. As we shall see in the last part of this section, there was another mode of poetic engagement which did not immediately translate this acute sense of one's mortality into an "affect". Rather, transforming it into the poetic metaphor of "making", it proposed the Renaissance equivalent of the ancient idea of *techne* engaged in the 'fantastic operation of the imagination (or a *mania* of the soul)' to produce new "worlds" (Mazzotta 2001). It is this operation of "cosmopoesis" which transforms the mortal limitation of self-knowledge into fiction and the Renaissance fascination with nothingness into the phantasmagoric practice of the artists. It is the fiction of self-knowledge of poetry which becomes the ground and measure for the *conversation* of all the arts generated out of the intellectual melancholy of the naissance. But before we can enter this complex relation between melancholy and an idea of "cosmopoesis", let us first quickly try to elaborate the nature of this intellectual melancholy.

Melancholia Generosa

The most systematic treatment of the problem of melancholy in the 15th century is perhaps found in the works of the Florentine neoplatonist Marsillo Ficino. But Ficino was more than a mere Renaissance humanist. As a translator and authority of Plato, he described himself as *Philosophus Platonicus, Medicus et Theologus* who practiced astral medicine and Christian neoplatonic mysticism as part of the same logic of universal harmony. And it is in this speculative creation of a totalizing hierarchy of creation that we find the contours of a theory of melancholy which borrowed from ancient humorology, as freely as it based its assumptions on neoplatonic astral magic. However, in essence, Ficino's cosmic model still followed the Ptolemaic version of a celestial harmony mirroring a terrestrial order. Ficino was not the first to point out the influence of the stars, particularly Saturn, in producing melancholy both as a disease and a temperament. According to an ancient tradition of humoralism which was founded on the basis of its relation to natural philosophy, at the latest by the 5th century BC, the effects of the stars—particularly that of Saturn which was considered cold and dry like the melancholy humor (black bile)—was considered responsible for the affliction. Since the beginning the pathological state of melancholy has been argued to be caused by an imbalance of the humors. Ficino, however, gave a new impetus to the astrological relation to humoralism in the early Renaissance environment where the intellectual and religious bonds, which held Europe together for more than a millennia, were coming loose. The rise of astrology, which was considered with much suspicion within Christian medieval moral-theological environment, gained precedence like never before. Ficino's neoplatonic mysticism has to be seen in this light when in the same book where he put his most systematic ideas on melancholy—*Three Books on Life*—he also talked of the sympathetic attractions, and accords that not only held the cosmos together as a single functioning organism but was animated by an aesthetic-musical concordance. Here music functioned as a form of living spirit which brings about cosmic harmony. It is strictly in this aesthetic context that we have to analyze Ficino's speculations on melancholy.

Ficino argues that there are three reasons for melancholy—cosmic, natural and human. All these reasons are related to intellectual labor. Saturn, which is responsible for the sustenance of the life of mind, is also a cold and dry planet that increases the melancholic humor. But it is in his construction of the natural and human causes of melancholy that Ficino's brilliance shows most prominently. According to the Florentine, speculation always entails an act of withdrawal—a recollection of the soul returning to itself from the outside world. And while one speculates it must be maintained, immovably, at the very center of man. This operation is analogous to an inalienable property of Earth which is constantly collecting itself from the circumference to the center. As a result the earthy humor—black bile—becomes activated which is responsible for inciting 'the soul both to collect itself together into one and to dwell on itself and to contemplate itself' (Ficino in Radden 2000: 90). Once the soul reaches its center, because it is also analogous to Saturn (which is the highest of planets), bile also induces 'the contemplation of whatever is highest'. As a result, 'Contemplation itself in its turn, by a continual recollection and compression, as it were brings on a nature similar to black bile' (Ibid). Finally, the human reason for melancholy is the generation of black bile because of contemplation where the brain becomes dry, and as it looses moisture (because moisture carries heat), it also becomes cold. This transformation is determined by the recollection and withdrawal of the spirit from the world into the self. Moreover it has to happen at the expense of some force which is generated by blood which in the process becomes corrupted and transforms into black bile. Therefore, Ficino writes: 'The more difficult the work, the greater concentration of mind it requires and ... the more they apply their mind to incorporeal truth the more they are compelled to disjoin it from the body. Hence their body is often rendered as if it were half alive and often melancholic' (Ibid).

Ficino, however, like many of his time (for example, Nicholas of Cusa, Pico della Mirandola and others), believed in the anthropological theory that the two basic human components—*corpus* (body) and *anima* (soul)—were connected by a third element described variously as *medium, vinculum* or *copula*. This *spiritus* was the connecting bridge between the corporeal and the incorporeal, which could influence both the "physis" and the "psyche" depending on its position. Moreover, this *spiritus humanus* corresponded to a *spiritus mundanus* which connected the material universe with the universe of mind. It is through this connecting element that astral qualities translated themselves into human qualities, and from the soul to the body respectively. The soul, however, was not *completely* subordinate to these astral influences. Only the lower part namely *imagination* (imagination) was mostly influenced. The higher parts, particularly *mens* (intuitive reason) remained essentially free. Moreover, by "exposing"[10] oneself to the particular star—through certain practices or using certain "medicines" or even astral magic—whose influence was causing negative effects on the subject, one could turn the negative effect into positive influence through a process of saturation. This theory of melancholy was, therefore, harnessed onto a prevailing idea of anthropocentrism in spite of its overt astrological implications. The pathology of melancholy could be turned into the generosity of thinking through the "work" of reason and, therefore, redeemed. The presence of astrological relation, in fact, reinforced this inherent anthropocentricism by highlighting man who as an active and thinking being could even manipulate the stars because of his freedom. As Klibinski-Panofsky-saxl remarks:

> ...thanks to this freedom (man could) harness the forces of the stars by consciously and willingly exposing himself to the influence of a certain star; he could call such an influence down upon himself not only by employing the manifold outward means, but also (more effectually) by a sort of psychological autotherapy, a deliberate ordering of his own reason and imagination. (Ibid: 270)

Such anthropocentricism, and its relation to melancholy, has been argued to be a specifically *modern* concern. It is said to be the reason for a consciously cultivated melancholy, which we find, for example, in Baudelaire's depiction of the figure of flâneur walking the streets of Paris detached yet reflective. Such a "modern" melancholic figure can be argued to be the result of the liberation of melancholy from the chains of pathology.

Marsillio Ficino is regarded as the liberator who elevated melancholy as a positive intellectual force, thereby, making it an inseparable part of the figure of genius. In this effort he is said to have revived a very ancient tradition prevalent among the Greeks where the close proximity between the melancholic and the genius was accepted as an evident reality. But in order to do so Ficino dissolves the distinction between the platonic idea of *mania* (as an unconscious access to truth) and Aristotelian idea of melancholy as a *potential* (for genius).[11] Moreover, following a later trend probably starting from Rufus of Ephesus, he categorized melancholy as the pathological *effect* of a life of mind rather than its *cause*. Moreover, the freedom of human will, which can overcome its melancholic condition effectuated by the stars and turn the stars to his own advantage to pursue a life of the mind (this is the project of Ficino), is distinct from Aristotle. The Aristotelian notion of melancholy unfolds as the contingent "medical" condition which provides the *potential* for genius which can only be actualized through a mastery of the self. Aristotle proposes something akin to an "organized anarchy" which has to be cultivated by the self as an ethical imperative to become a genius whose condition remains the melancholic humor. For Ficino, melancholy becomes essentially a cyclical operation. Produced as a by-product of the human capacity for free thinking, it can only be cured by the ingenuity of the free spirit.

Of course this attempt of Ficino to reinforce a doctrine of free will—through his concept of melancholy—has to be seen in the light of the intellectual background of his time. The *vita contemplativa* of the middle ages whose freedom was determined by a divine sovereignty was now replaced by a *vita speculativa* whose freedom seemed to be boundless because it declared the sovereignty of the human mind. But the constitution of such a sovereign logic of the mind was also paradoxically the condition for the possibility of its destitution. The autonomy of human reason which produced a new type of man, the *homo literatus*, also took man to the threshold of his knowledge where he became increasingly aware of his own limitations. The tragic *hubris* of such a life of mind was the *causa sui* of the growing *melancholia* produced by the sorrowful belief that grief and weariness are the constant companions of profound speculation. But this belief was not simply a result of the awareness of the mortal limitation of man. A growing anxiety seemed to have grasped the Renaissance imagination leading to the de-centering of this very autonomy of human reason itself. The effects of the Copernican revolution was not only far reaching into the future but was already anticipated in the intellectual environment of Ficino. It was an anticipation of the loss of heavens and the dislodging of man from the center of the universe which not only created an environment of melancholy but indicated the hitherto hierarchic ordering of thought replicating the universe as purely *metaphorical*.

As we have discussed before, the Ptolemaic cosmology supported an analogical principle of thinking that became the foundation of the medieval notion of a *vita contemplativa*. *Vita speculativa* however proposed to be a more complex phenomenon. In Ficino's magical-philosophical theory, as we have already seen, the symptoms of the loss of any external cosmological architecture which would support his meditations on a hierarchic ordering of the universe. His astral-theological-philosophical meditations on "above" and "below" already anticipate its illusory and relative nature. Jacob Taubes remarks that without being rooted in the external order of the cosmos *modern* theology and metaphysics, after the Copernican revolution would undergo a withdrawal becoming merely an *ordre du Coeur*. This act of being uprooted from having any basis in the external order of things which would counterbalance the internal moment of speculation made man's inwardness a purely metaphorical affair. The elevation of melancholy to an intellectual force seems to more or less co-inside with this loss of the heavens. At the basis of this "tragic" melancholy was therefore the withdrawal of thought on to itself without any analogical reference in the external order of things. The anthropocentricism of Ficino could be argued to be tragic precisely because it was only metaphorical. As we shall see—this metaphorical paradigm[12] of thinking "totalities" laid the foundation for an aesthetic consciousness which perhaps evokes the true singularity of Renaissance thinking.

However, for *vita speculativa* such "loss" spelled out the possibility of negativity as the fundamental condition for thinking. Hans Blumenberg in his tour-de-force *The Genesis of the Copernican World* rightly assumes that the rational anthropocentricism that Copernicus was to uphold evoked an autonomy of thought which no longer made possible for man to read nature as a pre-given text that he can readily interpret drawing on his Ideas and concept. The autonomy of man also meant the autonomy of nature which could now only be speculated on the basis of acknowledging the gap which separates them. Copernicus's famous statement in his dedicatory forward of *De Revolutionibus* testifies to this new speculative spirit. Copernicus famously argued here that his location at the remotest corner of the earth does not hinder him from dedicating it to the Pope who embodies the centrality of the public sphere 'so that learned and unlearned alike may see' (quoted by Blumenberg 1987: 38). The separation of his position (remotest corner) from the centrality of the public sphere does not impede or block the process of dissemination of knowledge and the cultivation of reason.

On the contrary, as Blumenberg points out, Copernicus compares his situation with the human capacity to think of the stars.

> ...(in) this differentiation between his own position and that of a center for the public sphere, he reflects the cosmological differentiation between the parochial perspective of his terrestrial 'corner' and the central point of construction from which the universe cannot, indeed, be viewed, but can be thought. (Ibid)

The dislodging of man from the center of the universe made possible by a doctrine of heliocentricism which replaces a principle of geocentricism had far more profound consequences than merely restoring one center in place of another. The heliocentric doctrine opened up the universe to an infinite number of centers which practically declared the loss of the heavens. The loss of a stable idea of transcendence interrupted the rational anthropocentric formula of the intellectual capture of nature. The autonomy of reason implied the reciprocal autonomy of nature which could now be imagined only as something opposed to the former. We see here the emergence of a dialectical mode of thinking where the object of thought no longer required the support of nature to give it the required validity of truth. Blumenberg displays his brilliant insight when he argues that at this stage *vision* in its natural capacity no longer could be trusted for giving validity to the concept and was left only with 'the residual function of aesthetics' (Ibid: 40). Blumenberg's extraordinary insightful remark starts to make sense at this juncture when he writes : 'at this point the unity of theoretical and aesthetic vision, since the ancient world is shattered and in a way that, in spite of the Renaissance's attempt at renewing it, is final. Since, at the latest Copernicus, comprehending and enjoying can no longer be carried out in one act' (Ibid: 39).

We would like to add here that Ficino's magico-philosophical imagination of Man and Cosmos as a single unified totality was nothing more than an *aesthetic* attempt to restore this separation in anticipation of its imminent dissolution. Therefore, for Ficino, this unity remains fundamentally metaphorical. Under these circumstances the identification of melancholy with that of intellectual speculation provided Ficino the way to extract enjoyment out of comprehension only through transforming the tragic state of man's alienation as the very object (aesthetic) of narcissistic enjoyment. Melancholy becomes symptomatic of the type of man who becomes the measure for everything but falls sort of himself. It is not perhaps till Hegel that we find a conceptual resolution of this problem of speculative thinking when the master philosopher devices his triadic mode of dialectic, thereby overcoming and yet preserving this negativity while simultaneously offering a new system of totality.

The Artistic Absolute

Before we conclude this section we would like to point out another trajectory which develops as a result of this Copernican loss of the heavens and the de-centering of man. This is a continuation of the metaphorical paradigm of Renaissance thinking which founded its ground on the basis of a relationship between melancholic desire for totality and the poetic desire for imagination. Giorgio Agamben perceptively argues for this relation between melancholia and phantasmagoria on the basis of a certain dialectic of desire. In his attempt to trace the melancholic genealogy of the Western artistic consciousness, Agamben argues that such consciousness is based upon the possession of its object on the very ground of its loss. He manages to show how the structure of phantasm, genealogically speaking, allows the artistic consciousness to emerge as completely self-sufficient because it coincides with the structure of melancholy based upon the conscious capture of the world on the very ground of its impossibility to be grasped. In other words, the very loss of the objective reality of the world becomes a reality in itself in the work of artistic imagination. From our point of view we can say that the metaphorical paradigm of Renaissance thinking gains its "reality" in the imaginary and fictional world of artistic expression. It is from this perspective that we should see the melancholy which informs Ficino's construction of a cosmic unity being displaced by the manic euphoria: Giuseppe Mazzotta calls this Renaissance experiment of world-making as "cosmopoesis" (Mazzotta 2001). As the world lost its authentic support in an external cosmic order, it came to occupy the place of imagination, whether that be the mad world of Don Quixote or the magical *theatrum mundi* of Prosperro in his island. The work of art becomes the emblem of the human world which perhaps explains its centrality in Renaissance imagination. It was not the optimistic magico-aesthetic construction of a harmonious but tragic world-order: a structure where melancholy as divine-mania functioned as the vehicle of transcendence of material reality. Mazzotta painstakingly analyses such Renaissance writers like Poliziano and Ariosto to show that the anthropocentric cosmos of Ficino is challenged by these writers who not only expose man's separation from nature but his incapacity to discern the nature of his own passions and manias. Poliziano, for example, portrays this equivocity of the platonic *furors*—in his *La fabula di Orfeo* (*The Fable of Orpheus*)—as not only deceptive but capable of producing such self-destructive energy which cannot be contained by Orpheus leading to his annihilation. This discordance, which madness unleashes, not only sits at the heart of life process but strangely enough has the structure of play. For example in Ariosto's *Orlando Furioso,* the *furore* of erotic passion effectuates a loss of objective reality of the world resulting in Orlando's *withdrawl.* However such a retreat into the self does not produce any profound speculative revelation. Orlando's erotic withdrawal becomes the elusive passage to a chimerical world of fantasy and figuration leading to his forgetfulness of virtue. As Mazotta remarks, it is the point where 'madness takes over' (Ibid 39). But this madness which is without any voice and therefore without language (Orlando loses his voice in his grief), nevertheless, becomes the condition of possibility for the construction of a world of play—the world of play as it is incarnated by the poetic imagination. But as Mazzotta points out 'for Ariosto play is nothing less than an *optics*, a certain manner of looking at the world' (Ibid: 45).

Leon Battista Alberti in his *On Painting* (1435) gives the theory of perspective—which will dominate modern artistic consciousness—through the aesthetics of geometry categorizing painting as the art of Narcissus. Alberti argues that for painting to depict an object, not as they are but as they appear to the spectator's vision, it has to be imagined as a triangle in such a way that it becomes clear that a very distant quantity should not be larger than a point. Alberti further explains, manipulating the etymology of the word "history" signifying in Greek "I see" (*historeo*) that a painting always narrates a history-telling how the parts fit the whole. Perspective is the art of fitting the parts together to give you the whole picture. Yet the irony of such totalizing vision is that it comes at the cost of certain narcissism. The evocation of the myth of Narcissus, who according to Alberti invents the art of painting, implies that perspective will always carry this paradox that in seeing the world the eye sees only itself. Perspective de-realises the world because in the final analysis it is an optical illusion. But the reality of this illusion is the reality of artistic expression which is the world producing. It is this double binding of perspective and its intimacy with the structure of play that becomes the new aesthetic principle which comes in place of a unified theoretico-aesthetic imagination. But the relativity of this vision—the impossibility to absolutely distinguish the truth from falsity, history from myth—produces a phatasmagoric worldview which subsumes all other subjective views making them intelligible from its own perspective. As Mazzotta notes: '(a) sense of contingency of life presupposes the vantage point of an absolute experience' (Mazzotta 2001: 47). This is the absolute of the poetic imagination, conditioned by a phantasmagoric ground, which is completely self-referential. It does not merely expose the irony of relativity but presupposes a secret access to nothingness, giving body to the incorporeal and making possible the construction of new worlds. Mazzotta points out, with precision, that in the end the Renaissance fascination with "making" discloses, as Pico della Mirandola had argued, the lure of an epoch seduced by perception-of-nothing. No wonder in *The Tempest*, we encounter Prospero, the conjuror of worlds in an alien island, who makes his exit with these lines:

> Now my charms are all o'erthrown,
> And what strength I have's mine own,
> Which is most faint (Shakespeare 1911: 66).

With these words Shakespeare not only testifies to the desperate mortality which clings on to Prospero's *vita activa* but clarifies the meaning of the world-making or life as theater. The genius of Shakespeare was not only to recognise the tragic melancholy induced by the unfulfilment of all desire but something more profound. It was to elevate theater as the metaphor of *cosmopoesis* or world- making such that one does not fail to understand that 'making is the mask of non-being or nothing' (Mazzotta 2001: 74). If *vita speculativa* falls victim to the melancholic consciousness of human frailty, the poetic imagination transforms it into *vita activa,* constructing whole worlds on the very ground of such groundlessness.

Conflict of Ambiguities

It is well known that Freud once famously remarked that his discovery of psychoanalysis remains the third narcissistic wound deployed by science onto mankind, the Copernican revolution being the first. Taking this as his point of departure, Jean Laplanche in his essay 'The Unfinished Copernican Revolution' (Laplanche 1999: 58) develops the following provocative thesis:

The Freudian discovery of the Unconscious was indeed a revolutionary *cut* in the history of human knowledge akin to the Copernican revolution. Like the Copernican revolutionary thesis of a de-centered cosmos (which was locked in a dialectic battle with the counter-revolutionary Ptolemaic tendency of a centered cosmos), so is the Freudian thesis of a de-centered and alien unconscious always struggling with the revisionist tendency present within Freud himself: that of re-assimilating this alien unconscious into the logic of a centered consciousness.[13] Laplanche argues that in psychoanalysis since everything practically begins with Freud, the revolutionary Copernican moment (decentering) and the counter-revolutionary Ptolemaic tendency (recentering) are present *simultaneously*. He further goes on to argue that the thesis of an unconscious as an internal other—inexhaustible and decentered—can be diagnosed at various moments in Freud's work: this, according to Laplanche, revolves around the following points.

1. The primacy of method : Instead of having any *a priori* concept of the unconscious or even identifying the unconscious from any objective proof from which a theory is extracted, Freud employs 'association and cross referencing' (Ibid: 61) resulting in a deconstruction of "analysis". Such a process where the object and its analysis reciprocally complement each other is without any direct correspondence. Hence a derivative hermeneutic operation, where conscious sequences can be identified corresponding to its unconscious signification, is rejected.
2. A realism of the unconscious: the object searched for leaves its trace on conscious scenes and fragments in a dynamic fashion—at an everyday banal level—where conscious tendencies are mixed with those deriving from the unconscious. The symptom is not a mere translation of unconscious because conscious discourse is not *analogous* to unconscious. This again leads to a hermeneutic impasse.
3. The general nature of symptoms—memories, fragments, scenes—is primarily sexual because sexuality opens onto the problem of the other.
4. Irrespective of the controversy of the causality of the unconscious—whether it is the cause or effect of repression—it has to be acknowledged that trauma from the point of view of treatment is always an effective causality in so far as it is *present*. It is like a "foreign body" (Ibid: 65-66) which enters from somewhere else rather than revealing something which is present *a priori*.

However, all these tendencies of acknowledging the alien-ness of the unconscious are constantly been subverted in Freud through such concepts as that narcissism, repetitive compulsion or even the "primary process". We do not have the scope to go into details of these tendencies now but suffice it to say here that they are primarily devoted to reduce the alien-ness of the unconsciousness by trying to either assimilate this alien-ness under the idea of a consciousness which is seen as more 'inward than my inwardness' (Ibid: 68). The same operation is at work in calling the unconscious *pathological* because it finally leads to the idea of the normal conscious subject who can master the unconscious and overcome its sickness. All these Ptolemaic instances of domesticating the alien-ness of the unconscious by re-integrating and re-establishing a vanished center can finally be overcome if we, according to Laplanche, go beyond Freud in order to fully realise his revolutionary essence and claim the double nature of this decentring. Following Lacan, Laplanche argues that 'a realism of the unconscious' (Ibid: 63) dictates that we think of an external guarantor of the internal other—an external other which only can maintain the primacy of the alien-ness of the unconscious. Laplanche famously emphasises here the theory of seduction and its relation to 'the existence of the other person' (Ibid: 73). It is, however, not in the alterity of the other person but the otherness maintained in language—which is further understood as the (Ibid: 74) 'category of the message' –that an external other comes to exist. Through his theory of seduction and its relation to language, Laplanche comes to a *theory of sign* which does not privilege the isolated centrality of the perceiving subject: this latter moment is what Laplanche calls the "index". While an index functions in a completely external fashion establishing an extrinsic relation with the signified privileging the perceiving subject, a sign functions in a doubly linked fashion. A sign gathers its force when the sender *makes it into a sign* through isolating it and addressing it to the subject. In other words, the message is always a *method of seduction*. It is always the external otherness which isolates and directs the sign to the self in order to guarantee the alien-ness of the unconscious. The external alien-ness is in turn maintained by its relation to its own unconscious—its own internal alien-ness. This is the inexhaustible potential of a constant decentering which is the true legacy of the Copernican revolution manifest in Freud.

From this point of view if we analyse the Freudian text of 'Mourning and Melancholia', we are unable to ignore the tension between the Copernican effort to theorize melancholy on the basis of an epistemologically inexhaustible unconscious and the Ptolemaic tendency of finding a narcissistic closure to this opening up of the self to the alien-ness of the unconscious. As we know, Freud's definition of mourning is a classic example in psychoanalysis of the domestication and recentering of the ego. The object of loss—most often through death—is identified along with every node of cathectic attachment in memory. Next, with a considerable expenditure of libidinal energy the ego is subjected to a detachment from the object. The work of mourning successfully allows the libido to detach itself from the lost object and invest onto another thereby re-establishing the ego in its place. As Freud writes: 'The fact is, however, that when the work of mourning is completed the ego becomes free and uninhibited again' (Freud 1959: 154). This Ptolemaic recentering of the ego—dislodged by the loss of the object of desire—is recognised by many as indicating a concept of work as against the worklessness of the process of melancholy. Someone like Ilit Ferber identifies in Freud this difference between the work of mourning which re-produces the ego as against the worklessness of melancholy which maintains the ego in its state of loss (Ferber 2013: 57-59). This, for Ferber, is the inadequacy of the theory of melancholy in Freud as compared to someone like Walter Benjamin who sees in melancholy a concept of productive work (aesthetic production) thereby emphasising its positive and non-pathological function. However, the reality of the Freudian analysis of melancholy seems to be much more complex than a simple distinction between work and its absence based on a productive logic.

All through this text Freud never shies away from using such phrases as the "work of melancholy".[14] But the nature of the work of melancholy is more complicated than mere re-production of the ego. Firstly, in the case of melancholy there is a distinct problem of knowledge of the object of loss. Unlike mourning, in melancholy, the person is not exactly aware of what she has lost. Freud writes: 'In yet other cases one feels justified in concluding that a loss of the kind has been experiences, but one cannot see clearly what has been lost' (Ibid: 155). Lacanians, like Žižek, have immediately identified here the difference pointed out by Lacan between the object of desire and the object-cause of desire which is constitutively lacking in the structure of desire. Melancholy is, therefore, the translation of the constitutive lack of desire into the loss of the object of desire.

The object is preserved as an object of desire in its very loss. We, however, are concerned with the decentering of consciousness facing a loss whose knowledge is not provided to it except as loss itself. Through melancholy the alien-ness of the unconscious becomes manifest while the Other (object cause) of desire translates itself into the object of loss. This perhaps explains Agamben's perceptive thesis that melancholy is not simply the failure of the work of mourning and the persistence of the attachment to the lost object but also the paradox of a desire to mourn even before the object is lost[15]. It is as if one is conscious of the constitutive futility of desiring an object even before the object is lost. It is in this sense that in Freud we find the question of melancholy elevated to the very threshold of knowledge. Melancholy is that shadow cast onto the conscious mind which carries the trace of the abyss beyond.

We see this problem of knowledge affecting the melancholic in more intricate fashion. One of the reasons why the melancholic's self-criticism cannot be merely seen as the work of her conscience is because of the incongruity between the knowledge of guilt and the actual guilty act. This amplification of self-deprecation which can even result in the loss of the "reality principle" is attributed by Freud to the pathological condition of melancholy caused by a conflict of ambiguities. The loss of the object which regresses into a loss of the self is sustained by a love-hate relation with the object which becomes directly related to the love-hate relation with that part of the ego which is identified with the object. As Freud writes:

> Thus the shadow of the object fell upon the ego, so that the latter could henceforth be criticised by a special mental faculty, like the forsaken object. In this way the loss of the object became transformed into a loss in the ego, and the conflict between the ego and the loved person transformed into a cleavage between the critizing faculty of the ego and the ego as altered by the identification. (Freud 1959: 159)

This leads us to the question of narcissism and the regression of the libido into the self whereby a part of the self is identified with the lost object on which the libidinal energy now focuses. It is here in his identification of melancholy with narcissistic regression, which

Freud relates to a primal narcissism, that we lose the radical effort to de-center the ego through a rupture which comes as a result of its encounter with the Other. The narcissistic closure comes early in Freud's text when he emphasises the unrecognizability of the problem of melancholy as the pathological moment *par excellence*. Moreover, Freud argues that the question of loss and the entire process of melancholic preservation of this loss (without any symbolic resolution and recentering of ego) is nevertheless triggered by a constitutive *identification* of the ego with the object-cause of desire. This is nothing but essentially a Ptolemaic effort to reduce the alienness sustained in the theory of melancholy by assimilating it to a narcissistic logic of a consciousness which can be identified behind the unidentifiable lost object. This effort is poorly *sustained* in the article 'Mourning and Melancholy'. The narcissistic centeredness is again destabilised and decentered when Freud acknowledges the inability to *fix* the origin of such conflict of ambiguity because the function of melancholy is to block any knowledge of the origin or sources of the trauma. The trauma is effectuated only through its presence in the symptom. Freud therefore writes : 'Thus everything to do with these conflicts of ambivalence remains excluded from consciousness, until the outcome characteristic of melancholy sets in' (Ibid: 168).

We return to our introductory problematic. It is evident that the question of a radical negativity is central to Freud's revolutionary discovery of the unconscious and its ex-centric nature that is also evident in his thesis on melancholy. However, the counter-revolutionary threat of a narcissistic closure on to a centered self is always looming in the Freudian discursive field. Melancholy in this sense can very well be taken as an index of perception of our post-modern reality where the subject in its narcissistic regression closes in-on-itself as the isolated source of all significations. The subject starts to maintain a completely extrinsic relation with its reality (signified)—even resulting in the loss of reality—because identifying itself as the origin of all significations it remains alienated from the perceptual whole. This is the narcissistic closure of a world destroying tiredness that Hans chul Pyong cautions us against. But we can also argue that such a counter-revolutionary condition of a melancholic perception is a "ptolemaism of the human psyche, its narcissistic recentering" which "follows upon a *Copernican stage as its pre-supposition*" (Laplance 1999: 83; italics mine). To decipher in the suffering body of the melancholic a concentration of existence (which bears the trace of a reminiscence that is not her own but comes from elsewhere) has been the great artistic quest since Renaissance. The artistic absolute of the Renaissance carries this value of *extravagance* that is like a pseudo-memory, cut off from its context, coming from elsewhere. Today we need to abandon the experience of melancholy as the perception of an artistic absolute and embark on a new search of the meaning of melancholy. The concept of melancholy as a *sign*—more specifically a cultural sign—which is exclusively meant for us by an alien sender in order to seduce us to a life of narcissistic passivity which is at the same time hyper active: such perhaps are the conceptual co-ordinates for this new journey which is only a continuation of a very old one.

Notes

1. Han cautions against a culture of relativism and comparisons which is flattened into a logic of the same. With the vanishing of any concept of *atopic* otherness all *heterotopic* differences get inscribed on to the surface of capital as consumable differences (Han 2017: 1-2).
2. In a yet to be published article titled, 'The Ambiguous Debt of Counter-Revolution to Revolution: Reply to a Vigilant Melancholic' Soumyabrata Choudhury has used this "tautological" term—because a Freudian concept of melancholy presupposes an inherent narcissistic tendency—to *emphasize the nature* of the melancholic tone of the current world order. In spite of being categorized as a pathological disorder, depression today enjoys the privilege of being a "normal" abnormality which you cannot do without as if it is to be narcissistically enjoyed.
3. Poorly translated as "sloth" this reduces the complexity of its medieval significance. The earlier spelling was *acedia;* later it became *accidia. Acedia* in Greek signifies a "non-caring" state (Radden 2000: 69).
4. In his letter to his protégé Stagirius, John Chrystom calls the malady by this name, evoking a general tendency of associating the problem of *accidie* with the monastic form of life which demanded a certain voluntary withdrawal from the affairs of the world (Klibansky et al 1979: 76).
5. The whole set of interconnected maladies known in the medieval religious-medical

literature as *filiae acediae*—daughters of sloth—included *militia* (malice, ill will), *rancor* (resentment), *pusillanimitas* (the smallness of the soul), *desperation*(despair) *torpor* (stupor), *evagatio mentis* (wandering of the mind), *verbositas* (garrulity), *curiositas* (curiosity), *instabilitas loci vel propositi* (instability of place and purpose) and *importunitas mentis* (importunity of mind) (Agamben 1993: 4-5).

6. Cassian remarks that *accidie* came to be known as the noon-day demon because of its description in Psalm 91: 'Though shall not be afraid of the terror by night; nor by the arrow that flieth by day; nor the pestilence that walketh in darkness; nor of the destruction that wasteth at noonday' (Radden 2000: 69).
7. Though Agamben uses sources spread across the Middle Ages, from the Church Fathers of the early Middle Ages to the Doctors of the Church belonging to the scholastic tradition, his first and most extensive remains from Cassian. Moreover, he frequently emphasizes the problem of *accidie* as part of the patristic tradition (Ibid: 3-18).
8. Jacob Taubes, 'Dialectic and Analogy' in *From Cult to Culture: Fragments Towards a Critique of Historical Reason* (Stanford: Stanford University Press, 2009), 165-176.
9. William of Auvergne, contrary to Chrysostom, considered melancholy illness not as a trial beset by divine providence but as part of the divine grace which supplements the monastic life of withdrawal from worldly matters (See Klibansky et al 1979: *77).*
10. Ficino believed that all forms of remedies from medicinal to astral-magical, in the final analysis, followed the principle of *exposing* the subject to the influence of stars which was the cause of the malady. He thereby provided a systematic schema of bringing traditional medicine with astral magic (See Klibansky et al 1979: 268).
11. At the very beginning of his famous *Three Books on Life* Ficino writes: 'Aristotle confirms in his book on *Problems,* saying that all those who are renowned in whatever faculty you please have been melancholics". Ficino goes on to identify this Aristotelian notion of melancholy with the platonic notion of divine mania remarking "My author Plato in the Phaedrus seems to approve this, saying that without madness one knocks at the doors of poetry in vain". This identification of the platonic idea of divine mania with the Aristotelian idea of melancholy testifies to the remark made by Hans Blumenberg that "there was never a renewal of the ancient world; it was an invention of those who had rhetorically professionalized themselves in the role of its renewers' (Blumenberg, 1987: 35).

    In Plato divine madness (*mania*) is the prerogative of four things: poetry (Muses), mysteries (Dionysius), divination (Apollo) and love (Venus) because they all provide direct access to truth without any conscious attempt at speculation which is the prerogative of philosophy. It is symptomatic of the "ancient feud" between philosophy and poetry which is the basis of the platonic imagination of the distinction between philosophic contemplation of truth and artistic appropriation of the knowledge of truth. Aristotle however in his theory of melancholy, in *Problem XXX,* provides a completely different perspective of the basis of genius—

both artistic and philosophic. Though we cannot go into detail over this point, suffice it is to say here that while trying to produce a totalizing concept of genius which would include both philosophers and poets, Aristotle in his *Problem XXX*, devises a method of conceptualizing controlled abnormality. It is the abnormality of the melancholics –produced as a result of the heating of black bile which is also the cause of abnormal *talent*. As Klibinski-Panofsky-Saxl remarks that in Aristotle abnormal 'is a neutral conception, implying no more than a deviation from normal conditions or behavior in one direction or another, so that either a beautiful or an ugly face—and even drunkenness—could be called abnormal'. The naturally melancholic even when he was perfectly well, nevertheless, possessed the *potential* -- a special ethos— which made him fundamentally different from ordinary and normal men. The melancholic condition was always that of the "normally abnormal". It is in this light we have to understand the Aristotelian relation between the melancholic condition which is the potential cause of genius and its subjective mastery such that one must control the temperature of the melancholic humor at a mean so that it does not fall so low that one becomes vulnerable to its lethargic and debilitating effects. However it also should not become so high that one goes into a trance or complete raving madness. It is this double limitation in order to maintain a golden mean which is the true identity of genius which can only come as a result of a subjective mastery.

12. The metaphorical paradigm of thinking "totality" during the Renaissance can be seen in its various incarnations which continued throughout the 16th-17th century in the use of such metaphors like "theater of the world" (*theatrum mundi*), "the play of the world" (*De ludo globi*), "theater of life" (*theatrum vitae*) and even *Theatrum Scientiarum* and *Theatrum Europaeum*.

13. The Copernican thesis of a heliocentric cosmos was the *enunciation* of a lineage which not only would continue through Galileo, Kepler, and Newton up to the Einsteinian revolution but it brought into focus an alternative tradition of cosmology going back to the third century BC to Aristarchus of Samos who was perhaps the first to propose a heliocentric system. However this alternative tradition was always a minoritarian epistemological trajectory in front of the majoritarian geo-centric model of Ptolemy. The Copernican revolution would not merely inverse this arrangement by gaining primacy while the Ptolemaic strain becomes minoritarian. The Copernican Revolution would *dissolve* this arrangement forever through the declaration of the opening up of the heavens. Jean Laplanche points out that the Ptolemaic system had many blockages, unexplained details which rather than questioning the system were integrated as *ad hoc* hypothesis which ironically came to support a cosmological system which was constituted on "an initial going-astray" (Laplanche 1999: 55).

In other words, beginning from a fundamentally wrong hypothesis the system strived to find or even invent elements which it had to assume in order to save the observable appearances in the movement of the planets. What is at stake in the Copernican revolution is the problem of the 'center' which does not imply a simple replacement of a geo-centric model with a helio-centric model. The thesis of heliocentricism opens up the universe for the first time to a logical and concrete understanding of infinity. As Laplanche remarks: 'The specific idea of heliocentricism was thus only the first step: the Copernican revolution, to some extent, opened up the possibility of the absence of a center'. A de-centered and infinite world was "wound" to mankind because it logically anticipated an epistemological break where man would not only lose his place at the center of the universe but cease to exist in his capacity of being a subject of knowledge. In other words, man would no longer be the central reference point of what he knows. From now onwards the Ptolemaic desire to re-integrate man into any logic of the centre would be a *counter-revolutionary* move which has to pay its debt to the Copernican revolution, so to speak. Kant's thesis of a transcendental subject and of *a priori* concept where the object conforms to the "constitution of our faculty of intuition" is clearly a counter-revolutionary Ptolemaic effort of recentering which however is declared *invoking the name of Copernicus*. I am indebted to Soumyabrata Choudhury for pointing out this dialectic between what he calls the "revolutionary hypothesis" and its counter-revolutionary strain (Ibid: 58).

14. Freud uses the term 'work a number of times while talking of both mourning and melancholy. For example he writes "it is tempting to essay a formulation of the work performed during melancholy on the lines of this conjecture concerning the work of mourning. Here we are met at the outset by an uncertainty' (See Freud 1959: 166-167).
15. Žižek formulates this hypothesis following Agamben's remark which he quotes 'melancholia offers the paradox of an intention to mourn that precedes and anticipates the loss of the object'. Žižek however re-affirms this formula through a Lacanian theory of desire as produced through a constitutive lack. Agamben however in his work marks this unknowability of the object of loss, in melancholy, as the threshold of psychoanalytic understanding of desire (See Žižek 2000; Agamben 1993: 19-21).

References

Agamben, Giorgio, *Stanzas: Word and Phantasm in Western Culture,* trans. Ronald L. Martinez (Minneapolis: University of Minnesota Press, 1993).

Buchner, Georg, *Complete Plays and Prose,* trans. C.R. Mueller (New York: Hill and Wang, 1963).

Blumenberg, Hans, *The Genesis of the Copernican World,* trans. Robert M. Wallace (Massachusetts: The MIT Press, 1987).

Ferber, Ilit, *Philosophy and Melancholy: Benjamin's Early Reflections on Theater and Language* (Stanford: Stanford University Press, 2013).

Freud, Sigmund, *Collected Papers,* Vol. IV, trans. Joan Riviere (New York: Basic Books, 1959).

Han, Byung-Chul, *The Burnout Society,* trans. Erik Butler (Stanford: Stanford University Press, 2015).

Han, Byung-Chul, *The Agony of Eros,* tran. Erik Butler (Massachusetts: The MIT Press, 2017).

Handke, Peter, 'Essay on Tiredness' in *The Jukebox and Other Essays on Storytelling*, trans. Ralph Manheim and Krishna Wilson (New York: Farrar, Straus and Giroux, 1994).

Klibansky, Raymond, Erwin Panofsky and Fritz Saxl, *Saturn and Melancholy: Studies in the History of Natural Philosophy, Religion and Art* (Nendeln/Liechtenstein: Kraus Reprint, 1979).

Laplanche, Jean, *Essays on Otherness* (London/New York: Routledge, 1999).

Mazzotta, Giuseppe, *Cosmopoiesis: The Renaissance Experiment* (Toronto: University of Toronto Press, 2001)

Radden, Jennifer ed., *The Nature of Melancholy: From Aristotle to Kristeva* (New York: Oxford University Press, 2000).

Shakespeare William, *The Comedies of Shakespeare*, ed. W.J. Craig (London: Oxford University Press, 1911).

Taubes, Jacob, *From Cult to Culture: Fragments Towards a Critique of Historical Reason* (Stanford: Stanford University Press, 2009).

Žižek, Slavoj, 'Melancholy and the Act' in *Critical Inquiry*, Vol. 26, No. 4. Summer (2000). 657-681

Zupancic, Alenka, *The Odd One In: On Comedy* (Massachusetts: The MIT Press, 2008).

Being, Melancholy

Huzaifa Omair Siddiqi

> In such a way hypochondria, considered as melancholia, becomes the cause for taking imaginary physical ills for something actual. The patient is well aware that these are imaginings, but from time to time he is unable to break loose from them...Melancholy(melancholia) can also be a mere delusion of misery which the low-spirited self-tormentor (inclined towards feeling wretched) creates for himself. In itself it is not yet a mental disorder, but may easily lead to it. (Kant 1978: 109–10)

> Nothing however can be more hideous than the figure of a melancholic, brooding over his imaginary misfortunes. (Pinel 1806: 136–7)

It may not at first seem strange to consider philosophy as a kind of melancholy, or at least as one of melancholy's effects. As a mood characterised by a fundamental withdrawal and retreat from philosophy's closure, melancholy typifies the contemporary repudiation of the Hegelian system. And as a fundamental *doxa* of contemporary philosophy this mood of withdrawal characteristic of melancholy transforms philosophy into a heroic[1] assertion of the opening, a refusal that calls forth the infinite possibilities of freedom. In Kant, however, there is a troubling revelation and a cautious admission that perhaps melancholy, that philosophical mood par excellence has the structure of a circulation around a disavowed fiction. What is most perplexing about such an utterance is its reflected resonance upon the discourse named philosophy which has always given pride of place to melancholy as one of its original and originary moods. In light of this we may wonder whether perhaps philosophy is, and always has been fundamentally attuned to melancholy, precisely because it has realised that the truth around which it circulates has the structure of a fiction. Does the perpetual melancholy of philosophy lie in its recognition of the eternal loss of truth? In this essay we will attempt to open up a space wherein the intense obsession and preoccupation of philosophy with melancholy can be placed contiguous to the problem of philosophy's uncanny fixation on the figure of fiction.[2]

By the late 18th century the discourse on melancholy had divested itself of all talk of bile, humours and astrological inclinations. With the work of Phillipe Pinel, one of the many founders of psychiatry, the clinical observation of signs and symptoms alone became the way to proceed with a diagnosis of mental illness. It is in Kant and Pinel we reach that moment in the history of the discourse on melancholy where it seemed possible to classify it firmly and decisively within one category of mental illness, namely the illness of the cognitive faculty. Yet as we can see above, in both Kant and Pinel there lingers a certain vacillation, ambivalence, and indecisive hesitation when it comes to melancholy. It is first of all a strange fact that we bring these two writers together to speak on this subject. The first is a philosopher of the limits of pure reason, unjustly infamous for never having stepped beyond the bounds of his town Königsberg (the stereotypical arm-chair philosopher if there ever was one); the second a distinguished physician with extensive medical and clinical experience in the field. Yet the question that they contemplate within the purview of their own completely disparate methodologies is simple: Is melancholy a real disease? The conclusion arrived at is startlingly similar: It is at the same time both real, and unreal. That a similar conclusion is arrived at by two leading intellectuals of two extremely disparate discourses makes the problem stand out as an even more startling one in the history of melancholy. What is even more remarkable is the inconclusiveness of their attempted conclusions, which in Kant actually ends as a complete denial of the intimate and ancient connection between melancholy and thought: 'In other respects it is a mistaken but frequently used expression to speak of a melancholy mathematician... when one means only a profoundly thoughtful person' (Kant 1978: 110). The indecisiveness of this decision is occasioned by the fact that both agree that the malady that the melancholic believes he suffers from are all imaginary and delusional. For Kant it is 'a mere delusion of misery which the low-spirited self-tormentor (inclined towards feeling wretched) creates for himself' (Ibid: 109); while Pinel more modestly describes it as 'the figure of a melancholic, brooding over his imaginary misfortunes' (1806: 136-7). It is not as if Kant and Pinel accuse the melancholic of deception or even worse, self-deception (for that would mean accusing him of being a *liar;* neither of the two, for obvious reasons, want to bring this problem within the purview of a certain juridical morality). Rather this is a judgement on the cognitive weakness of the patient, his inability to differentiate between reality and fiction (this inability to demarcate the actual from the fictional is not, as is usually considered, an external reflection, but the very internal condition of the possibility of fiction. There can be no fiction without a residue of undecidability about its status as fiction[3]). The patient is, in Kant's precise words, 'delusional', but not because he believes something that is manifestly untrue. The delusion lies in his inclination 'towards feeling wretched', in his inability to understand that his self-torment is quite evidently unethical towards himself. In point of fact, the melancholic demonstrates the greater incapacity to differentiate the realm of the imaginary from the actual. Perhaps this is why Kant cannot squarely place melancholy in the category of a disease (for one cannot be blamed for being ill, can one? There is of course a certain accountability of the melancholic for his condition, yet the paradox is that the subject of this accountability remains unaccounted for, as he is cognitively weak and thus cannot be blamed for his illusions. He is of course wholly accountable for having created and sustained his delusion, but not for having fallen prey to its seductive power).Thus both these writers accept the reality of melancholy as a cognitive weakness, but hesitate to categorise it as a disease. Though there is a separate qualification added here as well: in itself it is not an illness, but might easily lead to it. Pinel is perhaps more clinical here than Kant: 'Profound melancholia is frequently succeeded by actual derangements of the intellect' (1806: 139).

The problem with which these texts by Kant and Pinel confront us is not simply the nebulousness and indefinability of melancholy but the excessive care that both these writers take in their refusal to wholly categorise it, even at the very moment when the desire to classify (to give a semblance of order to these rag-tag bunch of symptoms and signs) drives their investigation. It is as if they both understand that there is something wrong with melancholy, some secret it conceals, a secret which is more a primordial fiction than a fundamental truth around which one must tread softly. It is only the intrusion of a new term, 'hypochondria', especially in Kant(and later in Benjamin Rush as well, a psychiatrist from America) which salvages the failure of this attempted closure of categorisation and opens up the discourse around melancholy to its own philosophical problems. Hypochondria is put forth as the defining structure of melancholy by Kant; this is agreed upon by both Pinel and Rush from the wealth of their medical and clinical experiences. Hypochondria: that paradoxical illness, whose very reality as a disease for the doctor is the patient's fervid belief that he is ill even though he has no symptoms of any illness–*except hypochondria itself.* Hypochondria is, thus, the exceptional disease because it is in all senses groundless and yet self-grounding; a disease that does not pre-exist but arises at the very moment of its (historical and medical) diagnosis.[4] While melancholy had long been considered a malaise that arises without sufficient cause, it might seem uncanny that Kant and Pinel draw a relation between it and hypochondria. But the very inconsistency of this medico-clinical diagnosis opens up for us a little crack in the door by which we can try to think the intense *groundlessness* (in all senses of the word, as without cause, as proceeding without condition, philosophically speaking; as 'groundless' as in the phrase 'groundless allegations') of melancholy, which means relating it once again to the discourse whose eternal shadow it has always been, philosophy. The melancholy of philosophy in many respects resembles this hypochondria, the excessive concern with the symptom and the chronic circulation of thought around one word or one idea.[5]

What cannot be doubted is that melancholy and philosophy have always been constant companions. In one of the earliest texts in the discourse, the *Problems,* Aristotle says that all creative people-philosophers, poets and statesmen—are essentially melancholic.[6] The work of the philosopher or the poet is supposed to be essentially melancholic as it keeps open the abyss of the origin of all conditioned existence without being able to appropriate its own conditioned being. Jacques Derrida's words on the work of mourning are characteristic of the immense weight contemporary philosophy gives to the work of melancholy:

> All work is also the work of mourning. All work in general works at mourning .In and of itself. Even when it has the power to give birth, even and especially when it plans to bring something to light and let it be seen. The work of mourning is not one kind of work among other possible kinds: an activity of the kind "work" is by no means a specific figure for production in general. There is thus no metalanguage for the language in which a work of mourning is at work. This is also why one should not be able to say anything about the work of mourning, anything about this subject, since it cannot become a theme, only another experience of mourning that comes to work over the one who intends to speak. And that is why whoever thus works at the work of mourning learns the impossible—and that mourning is interminable.Inconsolable. Irreconcilable. (Derrida 2001: 143)

This mourning—interminable, inconsolable and irreconcilable—is precisely the work of melancholy, melancholy which can never complete the work, and which always refuses the gesture of closure.[7] The opening is not just spacing but also the coming into being of time, the event of giving itself of space and time. Thus philosophy must forever work at the limits of this opening, at this gift from the event, infinitely, interminably and inconsolably.

Philosophy speaks the language of melancholy when it accepts that it is unable to give itself, unable to pay back the gift which comes from the opening. It is unable to integrate the opening within the speculative, within the law of the sublation and the system. For, as Derrida says, one can never really speak about this work of mourning. There is no metalanguage for this experience of the traumatic opening which can only make itself heard through the intense trembling, distortion and stammering of language. (But on a side note, let us also remember that all talk of *opening* is always in the language of the distortion of the field of meaning and symbolisation, a fundamental traumatic cut; one must keep in mind that the prisoners in Plato's Cave are utterly traumatised when they are brought out into the light of the Sun. It is, thus, apt that Freud in his essay 'Mourning and Melancholia' said that 'the complex of melancholy behaves like an *open wound*, drawing to itself cathectic energy from all sides' (2000: 290). Both philosophy and melancholy are obsessed with the preservation of this festering site, this open wound of thinking. It is in this way that we can understand the age-old connection between melancholy, creativity and the figure of the pained genius.)

This work of melancholy is supposed to revolve around the eternally lost object of desire which is the event of the gift of the opening. This work sustains the primordial responsibility to this loss, to this withdrawal which is also that of spacing and a *gift,* for it is by this withdrawal that the wound is kept open. We could thus be tempted to draw melancholy closer to the fundamental question of philosophy and the absolute abandonment; it would be an immense temptation to say that melancholy is primarily and essentially always the melancholy of finite beings abandoned by being.. Thus contemporary philosophy could hope to explain the groundlessness of melancholy, its sudden fits and starts, by its closeness to the other fundamental moods of Heidegger, anxiety and boredom.

What remains occluded by all these readings is the very simple fact, discerned so noticeably by Kant in his equation of melancholy with hypochondria, that both are essentially circulations around a certain delusion. The fictionality of this fiction is well known to the melancholic and the hypochondriac and yet, nevertheless, its effects remain resilient and cannot be dispelled. The assertion that melancholy involves a chronic and repetitive circulation around a fiction and that it stages this performance, does not mean to cast an air of moral judgement upon it or on the melancholic. That such a reading is usually presupposed is due to the fact that fiction (and need it be added, the lie) has not yet become a philosophical problem. It still operates on the margins of philosophy, as either a literary or an ethico-juridical issue. Perhaps it is through this examination of melancholy that we can bring the question of the fiction closer to its preliminary philosophical formulation. What remains unexplained and unexamined is firstly, the structure of this particular fiction: How does it function, what does it conceal, and why is its existence necessary? How does melancholy sustain its work if the loss it circulates is a fiction of its own making? Secondly, how can the revelation and unmasking of this fiction help us in understanding the essential and originary connection of melancholy with philosophy?

The remainder of this paper is divided in two parts. The first part seeks to reveal how melancholy is structured around the fiction of the lost object. The second part provides the preliminary observations on the intimate connection of this fiction of melancholy with the fundamental occlusion and amnesia of philosophy considered as metaphysics. It seeks to advance the idea that melancholy as a symptom indicates the *event* which always and necessarily escapes representation in metaphysical language.

Fiction of the Loss and Loss of the Fiction

In Ilit Ferber's book *Philosophy and Melancholy* the 'metaphysics of melancholy' (2011: 194) is brought within the realm of potentiality by the realisation that fidelity to the loss can never be reduced or subsumed within the work of mourning. Melancholy remains a moment of utter excess to the integrative law of subsumption, neither sublated and elevated into the work, nor transformed into the concept and the symbol. Ferber thus seeks to divest the discourse of its pathological, somatic, subjective, psychoanalytical and phenomenological inconsistencies and accretions. She hopes through a consideration of *mood* or *Stimmung* to position

> The discussion of melancholy in a sphere that is not merely psychological or subjective but also objective. This structure is central for establishing the connection between melancholy and philosophy and, following Heidegger, the way in which mood determines philosophy's encounter with the world. In this configuration mood serves as a (Heideggerian) opening and passage to the encounter with and expression of the world rather than, as sometimes conceived, as a contribution to the paralyzing closure from that world. (Ferber 2011: 14)

By destituting the discourse around melancholy from its keywords (pathology, the subject, etc.) Ferber's primary aim is to imbue it with certain objectivity. We must not be naïve enough to think that she desires a completely objective or clinical view on melancholy as a phenomenon. For what Ferber's book actually accomplishes is to uncover the suffusion of so called subjective melancholy in what we for long have considered objective: nature, being and time, especially through a deep reading of the work of Walter Benjamin. Ferber reads Walter Benjamin's work, especially his *Trauerspiel and Tragedy* as revealing the way one must take to unveil it as fundamental attunement to the world, similar to that of anxiety and boredom in Heidegger. It is commendable that Ferber does not hesitate in casting away its so-called 'subjective' aspects as it has long been considered in discourse, advocating it as a fathomless 'nonintentional'(in the Husserlian sense) attachment to an object which is lost, or, is not in fact objectively present. It is impossible to maintain an intentional relationship with such an object within the Husserlian paradigm, according to Ferber. She casts away the melancholic subject to unveil the structural suffusion of melancholy throughout what is called philosophy to bring the outdated discourse(based on somatic inconsistencies, pathological tendencies and subjective anxieties) more in tune with the Heideggerian analytic of *Dasein.*

The merit of Ferber's book lies in her uncovering of Benjamin's attempt to free melancholy from the metaphysics of subjectivity. For Benjamin melancholy must not be considered as 'intentional', as oriented towards a lost object, but as a linguistic mood of disclosure. It arises when man, whose linguistic being is to name things, *loses* that primordial naming language: 'losing the ability to name has thus caused man to lose his ethical responsibility toward nature instead of deepening it' (Ferber 2011: 139):

> Man's melancholy should therefore be understood as inner-linguistic, not psychological or subjective. Man is not sad or mournful for a specific loss relating to his subjective, contingent existence; his melancholy is linguistic, and it touches directly on his inability to execute his linguistic essence—that of naming nature. (141)

When man can no longer name nature he also fails to realise his own inner-linguistic potential, and thus there is not one loss but two. Language is deeply and profoundly tinged with melancholy because it is no longer the language that can name nature. It is not a specific loss but the loss of its very essence as language, its very *potentiality* as naming language which then deteriorates into the language of overnaming, propositions and idle chatter.

Here we can see the structural-philosophical suffusion of melancholy throughout nature and the linguistic being of man. The merit of Ferber's book is to demonstrate through the reading of Walter Benjamin's writings that melancholy is neither a subjective malaise nor a psychological failure of mourning, but rather is the name for a certain distortion in the texture of the inner-linguistic disclosure of language. This distortion is an essential distortion in and of language itself; and this distortion laments and calls for redemption. When distorted and torn away from its very essence and potentiality as naming, language gives way to lament and melancholy. It is as this distortion, this madness of the tearing asunder, that melancholy remains outside the integrative law of subsumption, forever carrying out its work as the gift of opening (for what is the *opening* if not this tearing asunder itself, this *distortion* of the entire field of being which is the event?).

It is within the purview of this insight that the nebulousness which surrounds the discourse on melancholy can be better situated. Can it not be said that melancholy names this distortion itself, a distortion in the very field of being which each epoch understands in its own way, sometimes as a somatic disorder, other times as a purely subjective affect, and in today's contemporary clinical discourse, as a mental disease?[8] However, it would be a fallacy to consider that it is only today we have realised that melancholy has the structure of a distortion. In fact we can quote two instances from English literary history where this idea is put forth in even more startling terms. Robert Burton in his magnificent *Anatomy of Melancholy* writes: 'The Tower of Babel never yielded such confusion of tongues as this Chaos of Melancholy doth variety of symptoms' (1824: 148).Burton here anticipates and precedes Benjamin, perhaps even exceeds him with his formulation of melancholy as the case of an immense linguistic confusion. Citing the Biblical example of the Tower of Babel is not only to evoke its intense untranslatability, but melancholy as the very field of untranslatability itself. It is not a distorted or mangled form of something (a language, a word, a thing) but is *distortion* itself, clouding and occluding the very field of intelligibility and sensibility with the immense profusion of symptoms. Around the same period as Burton, in Shakespeare's *As You Like It* the ramifications of this distortion and diversity is taken to its limits, where it can end up as nothing other than comic. As Jaques says to Rosalind:

> I have neither the scholar's melancholy, which is emulation; nor the musician's, which is fantastical; nor the courtier's which is proud; nor the soldier's, which is ambitious; nor the lawyer's, which is politic; nor the lady's, which is nice; nor the lover's, which is all of these; but it is a *melancholy of mine own*, compounded of many simples, extracted from many objects. (1993: IV:1, 11-16, emphasis mine)

Here, even within this comic mood we find a profundity of thought which is absolutely Shakespearian: melancholy is not just something that other people suffer from, and it is not just an impersonal mood. It is always 'a melancholy of mine own'; in fact it is melancholy precisely because it is one's own and can never be shared like grief or mourning. We are here not reverting to the personal/inner subjective discourse but revealing the truth of that discourse. Shakespeare makes melancholy almost a chemical formula, 'compounded of many simples, extracted from many objects'; in short an objective fact. Yet precisely here, in its very objectivity and in its structural suffusion throughout the entire body of human society, lies the utmost possibility and the necessity of a melancholy of mine own which cannot be shared and which cannot be collective or communal. In short, melancholy is a structural-philosophical horizon of disclosure, or what in Heidegger is called *mood.* Later on in the essay we will see, following this line of thought, how Shakespeare in *Hamlet* incarnates this mood as the distortion integral to the *spectrality* of the event.

Thus, it is not surprising that in his dense work *Contributions to Philosophy* Heidegger uses similar language when he brings up this question of the distortion that is melancholy, only to react against its traditional meaning:

> Care—it must be said ever and again- does not mean melancholy, preoccupation, or tormenting worry over something or other. All that is simply the distorted essence of care insofar as additionally it is placed into another misunderstanding according to which care is one 'disposition' or 'attitude' among others. (Heidegger 2012: 29)

Care in Heidegger does not name the emotion attached to someone or some object but rather for the field of care wherein we *project* our involvement with the world. Care is the word that in *Being and Time* for Heidegger names the 'structural whole of Dasein's everydayness in its totality' (Ibid: 226). Elsewhere Heidegger says:

> Dasein's Being reveals itself as *care*... if we are to work out this basic existential phenomenon we must distinguish it from phenomena which might be proximally identified with care, such as will, wish, addiction, and urge. Care cannot be derived from these, since they themselves are founded upon it. (Heidegger 2001: 227)

Heidegger goes back to the etymology of the word, tracing it back to the Latin *cura:* 'Burdach calls attention to a double meaning of the term 'cura' according to which it signifies not only 'anxious exertion' but also 'carefulness' and 'devotedness''. Thus care is the way Dasein can project itself, in its surrender to the world of concern or thrownness (Ibid: 243). With this conception of care Heidegger makes a break within the intentional phenomenological paradigm, and opens it up to its presupposed pure form of intentionality itself, which is always already non-intentional. 'Care, as a primordial structural totality, lies 'before' ("*vor*") every factical 'attitude' and 'situation' of Dasein, and it does so existentially a priori; this means that it always lies in them' (Ibid: 238).

Similarly Heidegger's suspicion of melancholy can be located within this book itself, as for example when he writes: 'The phenomenon of care in its totality is essentially something that cannot be torn asunder; so any attempts to trace it back to special acts or drives like willing and wishing or urge and addiction, or to construct it out of these, will be unsuccessful' (Ibid).It is in this sense that he criticises melancholy, preoccupation or worry over something. Such emotions are wholly intentional, and hence blind to the non-intentionality of the field of intention itself. While it is on the surface of it a powerful critique of melancholy in the traditional sense of a failure in the work of mourning the lost object, Heidegger's characterisation of it as a distortion of care opens up a new field of possibilities for thought. What if (and this is truly conditional) melancholy as a non-intentional mood of disclosure is a distortion of the fundamental attunement that is care? In that respect melancholy then becomes the name for a certain mood which is a primordial responsibility not towards a lost object or person but towards the very field of *loss* itself. As a distortion of care, it translates the structural whole of the everydayness of Dasein into the language of a primordial and originary loss, wherein care is restricted within the topography of the field of loss and cannot spill out of it. The melancholic is one whose care is restricted to the structural field of loss (and not as it is supposed, the lost object). It is in this way that we must understand melancholy as a distortion of care. In the melancholic the loss of care becomes the care of loss.

It is in the works of contemporary philosophy where this conception of melancholy as a fundamental responsibility towards the field of loss results in the prevailing dictum that one must be true to one's loss. Such is the attitude in many current disciplines, like gender studies (Judith Butler's 'Melancholy Gender/Refused Identification' is characteristic in this respect[9]), postcolonial studies and even queer theory. Slavoj Žižek is entirely correct when he writes that

> The predominant doxa is as follows: Freud opposed 'normal' mourning (the successful acceptance of loss) to 'pathological' melancholy (where the subject persists in his or her narcissistic identification with the lost object). Against Freud, one should assert the conceptual *and* ethical primacy of melancholy: in the process of loss, there is always a remainder which cannot be integrated through the work of mourning, and the ultimate fidelity is fidelity to the remainder. Mourning is a kind of betrayal, the 'second killing' of the (lost) object, while the melancholic subject remains faithful to the lost object, refusing to renounce his or her attachment to it. This story can be given a multitude of twists, from the queer one (homosexuals are those who retain fidelity to the lost/repressed identification with the same-sex libidinal object) to the postcolonial-ethnic one (when ethnic groups enter capitalist modernization and are under threat...they should not renounce their tradition through mourning, but retain their melancholic attachment to their lost roots). (Žižek 2001: 141-42)

The motto of the contemporary 'victim' culture we live in speaks the same language: One must be true to one's loss! One must be true to one's identity, which basically means being faithful to one's loss of identity (as a woman one has lost out something to the man, as a black man to the white man, as a Muslim to the Hindu majority etc.). Rather than trying to retrieve the loss (which in any case is a futile endeavour) identity politics today revolves around it, fetishizes it and nurtures the openness of the open wound. This might be a digression, but today almost every political faction speaks with this air of victimisation, has to appeal to this spectre of the loss, no matter that it might even be the strongest and the most privileged section of society.[10] The pure form of the loss must be preserved; the open wound must be cared for, where care means the preservation of the wound *as* wound.

Melancholy is thus the fundamental mood which characterises our present epoch, as a pristine responsibility to the myth of the lost object of desire. An extensive quote from Žižek would corroborate this point:

> For this reason, melancholy is not simply attachment to the lost object, but attachment to the very original gesture of its loss. In his perspicacious characterisation of Wilhelm Furtwangler's conducting, Adorno claimed that Furtwangler "was concerned with the salvaging of something which was already lost, with winning back for interpretation what it began to lose at the moment of the fading of binding tradition. This attempt to salvage gave him something of the excessive exertion involved in an invocation for which what the invocation seeks is no longer purely and immediately present." What one should focus on is the double loss that sustains today's (deserved) cult of Furtwangler...Furtwangler's passion was infused with a kind of traumatic intensity, a sense of urgency proper to the desperate attempt to salvage as part of our tradition what was already endangered...so what we are longing to recapture in old Furtwangler recordings is not the organic immediacy of classical music but, rather the organic-immediate experience of the loss itself that is no longer accessible to us– in this sense, our fascination with Furtwangler is melancholy at its purest. (Žižek 2001: 142-3)

It is this fidelity to the original f loss which is the defining characteristic of melancholy today. Almost all of contemporary politics today is melancholic because it hearkens back to the past, not to recover it, but to recover the immediacy of the loss which the past itself had suffered. In a way this melancholy of the political and the *polis* is doubly removed, doubly wounded, absolutely exiled from the lost object, and utterly false to it even at the moment of its authentic fidelity. Because the lost object, whatever it may be for these political imaginations (the traditional homogenous community set up for the white supremacists, the immediate organicity of the hierarchical caste system as imagined by Gandhi in his ideal village, the Salafist conceptions of the original *ummah*) is always already contaminated, mediated and infected by loss. The most that can be hoped for is precisely the political act of reclaiming the original gesture of *loss* itself.

However, this suffusion of melancholy is not restricted to the nostalgic, right–wing fundamentalists. It also infects radical academia and philosophy, precisely at the moment when philosophy attempts to carry out its work of interminable mourning. Hence a footnote from Reiner Schürmann's book *Heidegger on Being and Acting* which lays out the existence of this strain of melancholy in contemporary philosophy:

> Among the company of writers, notably in France, who today herald the Nietzschean discovery that the origin as one was a fiction, there are those who espouse the multiple origin with jubilation, and this is apparently the case with Deleuze. There are others who barely conceal their regret over the loss of the One, and this may indeed be the case with Derrida... For Heidegger, neither intoxicated jubilation nor mourning-there is only sober attending to the *pollakhoslegesthai* of the origin, a thinking more sober than scientific technology. (Schürmann 1987: 322)

Derrida is the one who is unable to complete the work of mourning (also a title of one of his most brilliant books), whose very style of writing is utterly melancholic(note the various ellipses, the immense number of qualifications, the disinclination to possess a definite place of enunciation or endorse a direct meaning, which is simply the reluctance to *possess* at all, and hence the reluctance to be *proper* and appropriative). Derrida seeks an impossible mourning, an infinite mourning, where the loss of the One can never fully be integrated within the symbolic order. It is this melancholic tremor of language, its infinite stammering and stuttering, which Derrida gives voice to. In *The Work of Mourning,* Derrida gives utterance to his own melancholy, at the funeral speech of Gilles Deleuze: 'I, the sole survivor of what has been identified as a 'generation'–of which I am the last born, and, no doubt, the most melancholic of the group (they were all more joyful than I)' (2001: 215). But it is imperative to read Schürmann's words carefully, even though this is just a footnote to his text, even though it might appear to be tangential to the proper focus of his book in question. For Schürmann quite clearly enunciates that what Derrida is mourning is in fact the discovery that the *origin as one was a fiction.* Derrida's mourning is precisely infinite, interminable and inconsolable because it mourns what is, and always was, a fiction. Revealing this fiction for what it is does not mean casting a moral judgement on Derrida and his work, as if it has for so long been prostrated in the worship of a false god and now can be led to the truth after the idols have all been smashed to pieces. The problem rather lies in the recognition of the excessive necessity of this fiction for philosophy. Why does philosophy, the discourse of the love for wisdom, revel in its circulation around the fiction?[11]

The strangest thing is that this infinite circulation around the loss as a fiction, which is melancholy at its purest, is completely saturated by the traces of an irrepressible and ecstatic joy.[12] That melancholy cannot be wholly separated from a certain enjoyment is an issue which finds many parallels in literature. Indeed the last stanza of John Keats' famous poem 'Ode on Melancholy' condenses in a few short lines the belonging together of the two:

> She dwells with Beauty– Beauty that must die:
>   And Joy, whose hand is ever at his lips
> Bidding adieu; and aching Pleasure nigh,
>   Turning to poison while the bee-mouth sips:
> Ay, in the very temple of Delight
>   Veil'd Melancholy has her Sovran shrine,
> Though seen of none save him whose strenuous tongue
>   Can burst Joy's grape against his palate fine;
> His soul shall taste the sadness of her might,
>   And be among her cloudy trophies hung.

This poem has in itself such a wealth of philosophical meaning with regard to melancholy that perhaps an entire essay could be devoted to it. Yet at this moment it suffices to point out that Keats' profound understanding that melancholy is not just infected with a certain aching pleasure of enjoyment, but rather it is itself the greatest enjoyment. This is not to claim that melancholy is just a masquerade and that the melancholic is just a masterful actor playing at being sad, deriving a perverse enjoyment from his own self-deception. On the contrary, it is enjoyment itself which has the structure of an intense and inconsolable melancholy. It is only a naïve understanding which believes enjoyment lies in the fulfilment of desire, when in fact true enjoyment (or, the Lacanian *jouissance*) consists in the preservation of desire through its non-satisfaction.[13] As philosophers since Hegel are well aware, *desire is always the desire of a desire*. Enjoyment and melancholy are born from a passionate concern with the death of desire, a death which must not only be postponed and deferred, but must also be simultaneously preserved to function within desire itself, invigorating it by the fantasy of its own demise. What animates both enjoyment and melancholy, right from the moment of their birth, is the sustained work that goes into maintaining the fantasy of their own end.[14] Žižek is thus correct when he says:

> In contrast, the fundamental maxim of the ethics of desire is simply desire as such: one has to maintain desire in its dissatisfaction. What we have here is a kind of heroism of the lack: the aim of psychoanalytic cure is to induce the subject to heroically assume his constitutive lack, to endure the splitting which propels desire. A productive way out of this deadlock is provided by the possibility of sublimation: when one picks out an empirical, positive, object and "elevates it to the dignity of the Thing", i.e. turns it into a kind of stand-in for the impossible Thing, one thereby remains faithful to one's desire, without getting drawn into the deadly vortex of the Thing. (Žižek 2004)

This enjoyment (in the terms of desire that we have been trying to articulate) animates melancholy in its tireless and chronic circulation of the fiction within the loss. The melancholic desires the dissatisfaction of desire so as to persist in its attachment to the fiction of the loss, which according to Žižek is a mode of circumventing the "deadly vortex of the Thing" which means a direct identification with the Thing(the impossible axis of desire) itself.

This unconscious enjoyment within the melancholic is revealed by Freud in his essay 'Mourning and Melancholia' to be caused by the simple fact that

> One cannot see what has been lost, and may the more readily suppose that the patient too cannot consciously perceive what it is he has lost. This, indeed, might even be so even when the patient was aware of the loss giving rise to the melancholia, that is, when he knows whom he has lost but not *what* it is he has lost in them… . (Freud 2000: 284-5)

Freud's essay is perhaps one of the most fundamental texts for the modern understanding of melancholy but it is strange that it is also the most misread text in the entire discourse, perhaps because of the misleading nature of the title. The driving force of the essay is not to actually differentiate and demarcate 'normal' mourning from pathological melancholy, even though that is how many readers of Freud approach it (and end up disparaging him for its degradation to the status of pathology). Freud's essay is actually an attempt to understand the problem of mania and its uncanny cyclical connection with melancholy. Jennifer Radden has documented how since the time of the European Romanticism, melancholy and mania were brought together in a cyclical system of affective complaints (2000: 15). She writes,

> the nineteenth century saw a renewed and more thoroughgoing development of the notion of cyclical conditions…PhillipePinel in 1806 asks whether melancholia of several years standing may not degenerate into mania, and he describes a 'thorough revolution of character' whereby those who were melancholic may eventually become 'maniacs'. In 1818 Johan Christian Heinroth interpreted Boerhaave to have held that mania was merely a more acute degree of melancholia…in 1854..Jules Baillarger and Jean Pierre Falret, independently proposed a new disorder…characterised by cyclical phases of both melancholic and manic states…known as *circular insanity* in England was to have a central place in the psychiatric nosology of the nineteenth century. (Ibid: 15-16)

Freud's essay follows up on this problem: how does melancholy, that disease of low spirits, inactivity and passivity, suddenly transform itself into highly active and energetic mania? In fact Freud's essay is intensely concerned with the question of defining 'pain in terms of the economics of the mind' (Freud 2000: 284). It is this violation of the economics of the mind which puzzles Freud so much about melancholy's turn to mania: 'The most remarkable peculiarity of melancholia, and one *most in need of explanation* is the tendency it displays to turn into mania accompanied by a completely opposite symptomatology' (Ibid: 290). It is this *economic* problem which Freud mulls over, unable to integrate this transference of symptoms and energies within the mental economics of pain. Firstly, (his argument goes) melancholy results in a suppression of cathectic energies for a long period of time, then when it ends then this 'bound' energy is suddenly made available, and the maniac, free from the object which had been the cause of his suffering, runs 'after new object-cathexes like a starving man after bread' (Ibid: 291). However, while such an explanation seems plausible upon first reading, it does not explain why the end of the work of mourning does not in any way result in mania. The same cathectic energy is repressed in both cases, yet why is the effect so different when it comes to melancholia? Freud's tentative response is that the answer must lie in the 'regression of the libido into the ego' which accumulates a tremendous amount of cathectic energy which is then released after the end of the debasement and rage of the ego against itself as mania. However, this remains an economic problem because loss of energy is suddenly transformed into an excess of energy. This cannot be answered by the regression of the libido into the ego as that too is not a conservative process but rather consumes an immense amount of cathectic libidinal energy until 'the fury has spent itself or that the object is abandoned as no longer of value' (Ibid: 293). It is pure economic common sense that Freud finds himself up against: a suppression of energy can release itself as mania, but then a similar process does not occur in mourning; the expenditure and loss of energy in the 'fury' of the libidinal regression cannot result in the generation of more energy. How is this problem, which is the true concern of Freud's essay, to be solved?

It is Giorgio Agamben who in his essays in *Stanzas* offers a solution to this economic problem by arguing that melancholy is not only the failure of the work of mourning but its opposite: 'the melancholy offers the paradox of an intention to mourn that precedes and anticipates the loss of the object' (Agamben 1993: 20). Agamben observes, with a certain bemusement that

> melancholy would be not so much the regressive reaction to the loss of the love object as the imaginative capacity to make an unobtainable object appear as if lost. If the libido behaves as if a loss had occurred although nothing has in fact been lost; this is because the libido stages a simulation where what cannot he lost because it has never been possessed appears as lost, and what could never be possessed because it had never perhaps existed may be appropriated insofar as it is lost. (Ibid)

This staging of the loss, this exhibition of the open wound is primarily a method for melancholy to appropriate what was never possessed, perhaps because it never even existed. This loss is staged and simulated to mark out the space for the unreal which 'the ego may enter into relation with it and attempt an appropriation such as no other possession could rival and no loss possibly threaten' (Ibid). Remarking on Agamben's profound breakthrough, Žižek writes the 'melancholic's *refusal* to accomplish the work of mourning thus takes the form of its very opposite: of a faked spectacle of *excessive, superfluous mourning* for an object even before this object is lost' (2001: 146). Perhaps Agamben's insight can solve Freud's economic problem: when the power of the fiction of the loss is unable to hold onto this energy expended upon the spectacle of excessive mourning, this excess energy is transferred (by the loss of the fiction of the loss) into the vigorous and vital activity of mania. But this is just a preliminary conjecture; the true answer might lie in even more obscure psychoanalytic mechanisms. However, the discovery that the loss around which melancholy revolves is a fiction opens up its innate and inherent appropriative nature. The need of melancholy to stage this whole fictional simulation is because of a certain inconsistency in its own structure: it fakes this spectacle of mourning a loss which can never be recuperated precisely because there has occurred an even more fundamental loss—the loss of *desire* itself. Žižek writes that the melancholic

> possesses the object, but has lost his desire for it...far from accentuating to the extreme the situation of frustrated desire, of

> desire deprived of its object, melancholy, rather stands for the presence of the object deprived of the desire for itself- melancholy occurs when we finally get the desired object, but are disappointed with it. In this precise sense melancholy (disappointment with all positive, empirical objects, none of which can satisfy our desire) is in fact the beginning of philosophy. (Žižek 2001: 148)

This is precisely the fiction which melancholy stages: not merely the fiction of the loss but the illusion that desire is still active, still present and still an animating force in the circular movement of the infinite drive which seeks the turning only so as to return to the same plane of operation.[15] It is here that melancholy can be seen as almost analogous to hypochondria in that both follow a similar mechanism of functioning. In hypochondria the lack of any symptoms is sought to be transferred and translated into the plane of disease by a very deft and ingenious manoeuvre. The hypochondriac can approach the doctor, who would perhaps be so kind as to rob him of his illusions of illness, by pointing out the nonexistence or misrecognition of his symptoms. Yet the hypochondriac move par excellence is this inventive gesture of re-appropriation. The hypochondriac will admit that he has no symptoms of any known disease: *except* hypochondria itself! This is the true and decisive *power* of the hypochondriac: he can never be proved wrong as it is he who is precisely the exemplary model of the Schmittean sovereign. It can similarly be shown that melancholy too harbours this spectrality by its gesture of generating its own spectral metalanguage through translation. At the heart of the misrecognition inherent in both phenomena there is a constitutive confusion between *lack* and *loss,* and a translation and transference from one plane to the other. As Žižek says: 'Insofar as the object-cause of desire is originally… lacking, melancholy interprets this lack as a loss, as if the object lacking were once possessed and then lost' (2001: 143).

Melancholy Philosophy and the Event

It is in this precise sense that Heidegger in his *Contributions* names 'the lack of a sense of plight' (2012: 185) as the symptom for the entrenchment of the abandonment of being where 'the lack of a sense of plight is, in a manner of speaking, raised to a principle' (Ibid). The abandonment of being, which should be the greatest plight, is not received as a plight at all. This is because being is not raised to the level of a fundamental question and it remains forgotten by philosophy considered as metaphysics. Truth is taken as an object of calculation, as if it is self-evident and the machinational understanding is the predominant one that provides the measure for all other thought. 'This claim has no necessity–it lacks the plight since it derives its apparent justification from the lack of a sense of plight' (Ibid: 260). The greatest plight is the fact that the plight of the abandonment by being is not received or understood as a plight. And this is Heidegger's precise formulation of the necessity of this extreme plight which requires a '*dislodging* of humans out of the lack of a sense of plight and into the most extreme plight, namely, the plight of lacking a sense of plight' (Ibid: 185).

It is, thus, that the extreme necessity of melancholy as a fiction of the loss is made clear to us. It is the truth that melancholy revolves around the fiction of the loss, yet what was perplexing was its intimate connection with philosophy as a discourse of the love of wisdom. Why would the pursuit of truth so constantly and necessarily revolve around a fiction? In Heidegger's terms we can understand the necessity of this fiction: for melancholy is the name of precisely *the plight of the lack of sense of plight*. The recognition of its loss as a fiction is not something external to melancholy, but is in fact its driving force. It is because melancholy instrumentalizes this 'lack of a sense of plight' and is the vehicle for its transformation into the utmost Heideggerian plight: 'The plight of a lack of sense of plight'. That is why the revelation of the fiction of melancholy does not in any way hinder its work; in fact it is melancholy which itself reveals its fiction, which wants philosophy to be stricken by the realisation of its tremendous plight of the lack of sense of plight: a plight which is profoundly *groundless*. As Heidegger says, this plight is the predicament of the abandonment by Being, which is not and can never be tantamount to the abandonment by any being, real or imaginary. Melancholy is the translation and transference of this *lack* into the (fiction of the) loss which is the only way that language concerned with beings (a purely metaphysical language) can articulate and give voice to the forgetting of Being. In this way it generates its own metalanguage, which is always already tainted with traces of spectrality. For melancholy to recuperate and recover this feeling of the lack of Being, the forgetting of Being (which is not an object or a being), means its staging of the fiction of the loss; the fiction which points towards its own fictionality and its concealment of the truth that there is precisely no reason at all for being melancholy. And that itself is the greatest plight.[16] It is in these terms that in *Spurs* Derrida read a fragment by Nietzsche that simply says: 'I have forgotten my umbrella' and in the postscript wrote:

> Thus in a thousand ways has the forgetting of Being been represented as if Being (figuratively speaking) were the umbrella that some philosophy professor, in his distraction, left somewhere. Forgetting, then, not only *attacks* the essence of Being inasmuch as it is apparently distinct from it. It belongs to the nature of Being and reigns as the destiny of its essence. (Derrida 1981: 143)

Being operates as the fundamental lack and the absolute abandonment; it hides itself in a veiled concealment (*verbogenheit*). The forgetting of being, thus, involves a preliminary forgetting of the veiled essence of Being itself. Being itself operates as a lack, as the lack which paradoxically is *given,* as Heidegger says by the 'and' in the title of the seminar *Time and Being:* '*Ereignis* is to be thought in such a way that it can be neither retained as being nor as time. It is to speak, a *neutrale tantum,* the neutral 'and' in the title *Time and Being*' (Heidegger 1977: 43). It is this neutral word, the 'and', which names the event of appropriation (*Ereignis*) which melancholy philosophy seeks to uncover and articulate within a language which is still utterly and absolutely metaphysical. The 'and' is the most melancholy word. As it is the word that gives Being and time, yet itself remains hidden and curiously *inappropriate.*[17] Melancholy's tortuous method of indicating the event of appropriation from within the language of metaphysics is closely related to the way the 'and' mediates between Time and Being in both *Being and Time* and *Time and Being.*

There is a strange little text, almost forgotten and passed over in the recent history of English literature, which speaks of a marvellous book, *The Book of Ands*. This short story (also titled 'The Book of Ands' and first published in 1984) by Robert Grossmith, is a parody of the classic Jorge Luis Borges story *The Book of Sand*. Though at times almost amateurish in its art, the story stages a profound reflection on the humble conjunction 'and' as the originary word. The short story begins with a wonderful cutting short of the first sentence of the Gospel of St. John: 'In the beginning was the word and'. The 'and' is the beginning of all things. As the name of the event it is and always has been the origin of all Being while itself remaining veiled in utter mystery. In the story the narrator buys a remarkable book from a salesman, the marvellous and mysterious *Book of Ands* written by a nondescript nonentity called George Lewis Berg. All paragraphs of the book are as follows:

> Andandandandandandandandandandandandandandandandand andandandandandandandandandandandandandandandandand andandandandandandandandandandandandandandandandand andandandandandandandandandand…

The narrator of this short story continues:

> I quote from memory the opening words of the Book of Ands. In the intervals between the conjunctions lies my story, lie all stories. I'm sorry, this is not the best way to begin. Let me try again. It is a convention of most stories these days to declare their own fictiveness. My story, however, is true. I live alone in a top-floor flat in a small university town in a universe expanding at both ends.

It is this *Book of Ands* which brings the narrator to the edge of depression, to a crisis of melancholia which arises from the infinite narratives concealed in this Book. As the short story progresses we see the divine nature of the book, its vast gaps and utter abscesses calling forth a multitude of stories from within the narrator, until he is almost driven mad, subject to the intense mode of what we may quite safely call melancholy. We can say it is melancholy because of its chronic circulation around one idea:

> Then it struck me. If my life could be written or read in so many different ways, if it contained so many different plots, as many plots as readings, did it not follow that it lacked any plot at all? The more I probed this thought, the more alarming it became. What was my life after all, but a random series of disconnected events, a chaos of discrete impressions strung by a memory on a necklace of conjunctions, assigned by a spurious structure to create this illusion of a unitary I? Wherein did the order of my life consist but in the momentary arrangement of the fragments of time into a notional pattern of sense, a pattern as arbitrary and ephemeral as the chance constellation of glass beads in a kaleidoscope? What was that famous whimsical definition of a net? A collection of holes held together with string. What was my life, what was the universe, but just such a net- a fabric of absences sewn together by thought, a chain forged by fancy, The Book of Ands made flesh.

Yet the lesson of this short story is almost Heideggerian. In fact, it condenses the entire object of this essay: that the narrator's melancholy arises out of misrecognition and a misreading of the fiction. He tries to fill up the gaps between the 'ands' and create a narrative but every attempt to do so leads him to utter despair and melancholy, an infinite circulation around the lost object which is fullness of Being embodied as meaning. Yet the necessary error the narrator makes is to read the 'ands' as separating the gaps when in truth the 'and' is the name for the gap itself, for the event of the gift which remains foreign and heterogeneous to the order of Being. *The Book of Ands* by George Lewis Berg is the text of a pure, unsullied melancholy because it embodies the spoken silence of the event, the *infinite stammering* (for this repetition of 'ands' seems to promise a new word each time, the opening which is a new language that can speak the Heideggerian 'other thinking'. Even though this hope is dashed every time, it is also renewed at the same instant) which is both the promise of difference and the infinity of repetition. Melancholy hovers around and feeds off this infinite stammering that is the event of appropriation, from within the language of metaphysics itself, and is not external to it or outside it. That is why it is a phenomenon that can be said to be transitional, even spectral, Janus faced, neither belonging to metaphysics nor to the other thinking.

Literature has always understood this essential spectrality of the fiction of melancholy, its function as an index towards a non-metaphysical language which from the terrain of metaphysics can seem only to be a profound silence. This spectrality is best given voice in the dying words of Shakespeare's Hamlet. Hamlet has always been considered the prototypical model of the Western melancholic. His entire existence in the play is in the style of an indefinite procrastinator, speaking with an infinite stammer where the words are always "out of joint" (1992: I:5, 190), unable to fulfil their meaning.[18] At the moment of his death, after having finally accomplished the long procrastinated act, Hamlet whispers to Horatio, in the most melancholic words of the play: 'the rest is silence' (V:2, 356). It is the silence of the event of death (which is the event that can never be my own, and hence is suffused with a primordially original melancholy) which Hamlet asks Horatio to hearken to, as it is this silence which disjoins and dislocates both time and being through its ineluctable and indelible traces.[19] To gift words to this silence is the impossible work that melancholy attempts even from within the limitations of philosophy considered as metaphysics. The structuration of melancholy as a fiction is saturated by philosophy's perpetual struggle to present this gift from the silence and its inconsolable desire to give language to this infinite stammering of the event.

Notes

1. Aulus Gellius, the Roman orator and grammarian had ironically declared melancholy to be the mood of heroes (Klibansky, Panofsky and Saxl: 1964: 16): 'thus it came about that, associated with the myths, the melancholic disposition began to be regarded as, in some degree, heroic' (Ibid.) The connection between melancholy and madness which persists even until Kant and Pinel is also derived from this heroism. This heroism is embodied in such madly *furious* heroic archetypes like Heracles, Bellerophon or Ajax who was cursed by the gods to lose their sanity. Thus it was perhaps apt that Cicero, the famous orator, translated *melancholia* as *furor* in Latin.

2. It would be tempting here to also speak of the spectral nature of the fiction and connect it with philosophy as a discourse around the simulacrum of the truth. However the word spectral does not wholly encompass the experience of the fiction as fiction. Perhaps a new terminology is desperately required for this phenomenology of the fiction. Can Heidegger's 'phenomenology of the inapparent' in his last seminars explain this schema? Perhaps, but only if we translate *unscheinbaren* as inconspicuous.
3. As Jacques Derrida writes: 'As we know, phantasma also named for the Greeks the apparition of the spectre, the vision of the phantom, or the phenomenon of the revenant. The fabulous and the phantasmatic have a feature in common: *strict sensu*, in the classical and prevalent sense of these terms, they do not pertain to either the true or the false, the veracious or the mendacious. They are related, rather, to an irreducible species of the simulacrum or even of simulation, in neither the penumbral light of a virtuality that is neither being nor nothingness, nor even an order of the possible that ontology or a mimetology could account for or subdue with reason.' (Derrida 2002: 28) The fiction is always spectral, but inapparently and inconspicuously so.
4. It might be fruitful to pursue further considerations on political theology and hypochondria. Is Carl Schmitt's sovereign thus the perfect model of the hypochondriac?
5. Jennifer Radden writes: 'Brudenell Carter, a 19th century authority on hysteria, speaks of a 'natural conformation' that causes women to feel, under certain circumstances, where men think, and builds on this allegedly natural division a proneness to hysteria in women and to hypochondria in men'.(Radden 2000: 28). Hypochondria represents thought gone awry, but as Phillipe Pinel writes: 'Melancholics are frequently absorbed by one exclusive idea, to which they perpetually recur in conversation, and which appears to engage their whole attention' (1806: 138).
6. 'Why is it that all men who have become outstanding in philosophy, statesmanship, poetry or the arts are melancholic?' Though it has been doubted whether the *Problems* was actually written by Aristotle or not (with some like Jennifer Radden (2000) attributing it to Theophrastus), the fact remains that in the larger melancholic tradition it has always been considered Aristotelian.
7. As Derrida continues in his eulogy: 'In the era of psychoanalysis, we all of course speak, and we can always go on speaking, about the "successful" work of mourning—or, inversely, as if it were precisely the contrary, about a "melancholia" that would signal the failure of such work. But if we are to follow Louis Marin, here comes a work without force, a work that would have to work at renouncing force, its own force, a work that would have to work at failure, and thus at mourning and getting over force, a work working at its own unproductivity' (Derrida 2001: 144).
8. Such an argument needs to be developed further but due to lack of space cannot be pursued here. However it is of extreme and urgent interest for us to investigate how each epoch manages to name its blind spot, its distortion, its *groundlessness*

in terms of melancholy, binding it each time to different causes, effects, and even symptoms.

9. Butler's idea is extremely influential in contemporary gender studies, positing that 'Heterosexual identity is purchased through a melancholic incorporation of the love that it disavows: the man who insists upon the coherence of his heterosexuality will claim that he never loved another man, and hence never lost another man. That love, that attachment becomes subject to a double disavowal, a never having loved, and a never having lost. This 'never-never' thus founds the heterosexual subject as it were; it is an identity based upon the refusal to avow an attachment, and hence the refusal to grieve' (Butler 1995: 139-40). However, what escapes Butler is that this disavowal is inherent to melancholy itself, and not external to it. Melancholy itself is a sort of disavowal which opens up the question of the stability of a field of study which has disavowed this crucial disavowal. Though Butler aligns her notion of performativity with gender and melancholia, she does not take this alignment far enough to posit that melancholy too is a performance.
10. Recent political developments have confirmed this. From the President of the United States of America to the privileged upper castes in India, all powerful factions seek to portray themselves as victims, even though they have concentrated all the power and privilege amongst themselves. This re-appropriation of the politics of melancholy in a new and virulent form by the ones already in power is one of the most dangerous developments of our times. In that way they can occupy power while at the same time believing they are powerless, and hence not responsible for their own misdeeds.
11. Derrida's essay 'The History of the Lie' in *Without Alibi* revolves around a similar question: the 'irreducibly ethical dimension of the lie' and the abyss that separates it from its political history (Derrida 2002: 29).
12. In 'Mourning and Melancholia' Freud quite aptly describes the lack of shame in the melancholic as a symptom where 'one could almost say that the opposite trait of talking about himself and pleasure in the consequent exposure of himself predominates in the melancholiac' (286) He also quite unequivocally says that the melancholic derives 'sadistic gratification from its suffering. The self-torments of melancholiacs, which are no doubt pleasurable, signify, just like the corresponding phenomena in the obsessional neurosis, a gratification of sadistic tendencies and hate, both of which relate to an object and in this way have both been turned round upon the self' (Freud 2000: 289).
13. Žižek writes: 'Desire is in itself "pure", it endeavors to avoid any "pathological" fixation. The "purity" of desire is guaranteed by the fact that desire resides in the very gap between any positive object of desire and desire itself—the fundamental experience of desire is "*cen'est pas ça*", this is not THAT' (Žižek 2004). Is this not the *purity* of the melancholic gesture? In *The Ticklish Subject* he extensively analyses the problem of desire especially with regard to what he calls the desire for unsatisfaction: 'desire reflexively desires its own unsatisfaction, the postponement of the encounter with *jouissance*—that is, the basic formula of the reflexivity of desire is to turn the impossibility of satisfying desire into the desire for non-satisfaction' (Žižek 1999: 291).

14. Here Žižek contrasts the standard perspective on Lacan's theory of enjoyment with its real implications: 'The predominant reading of Jacques Lacan reduces him to a kind of "philosopher of language" who emphasized the price the subject has to pay in order to gain access to the symbolic order—all the false poetry of "castration", of some primordial act of sacrifice and renunciation, of jouissance as impossible; the notion that, at the end of the psychoanalytic cure, the analyse and has to assume symbolic castration, to accept a fundamental, constitutive loss or lack, etc. To such an approach, one has to oppose its obverse, which is usually passed over in silence: the trouble with jouissance is not that it is unattainable, that it always eludes our grasp, but rather that one can never get rid of it, that its stain forever drags along—therein resides the point of Lacan's concept of surplus-enjoyment: the very renunciation to jouissance brings about a remainder/surplus of jouissance. This surplus-enjoyment complicates the problem of responsibility. The subject can exonerate himself of responsibility with regard to the symbolic network of tradition which overdetermines his speech; he is justified in claiming that "I am not the true author of my statements, since I merely repeat the performative patterns I grew into—it is the big Other which effectively speaks through me" (say, the author of a racist injury can always evoke the network of historical sedimentations in which his speech act is embedded). However, the subject is fully responsible for the little bit of enjoyment he finds in his aggressive racist outburst' (Žižek 2004). It is this little bit of enjoyment which we actually are trying to unveil here.
15. Walter Benjamin himself writes in a similar vein on the poems of Erich Kastner: 'Kastner's verses have forgotten all this. Their beat very precisely follows the notes according to which poor rich folk play the blues; they correspond to the *mournfulness of the satiated man* who can no longer devote all his money to his stomach. Tortured stupidity: this is the latest of two millennia of metamorphoses of melancholy' (Benjamin 1999: 426). Melancholy can very easily become the mask which hides the satisfaction and hence eradication of desire.
16. As Heidegger says elsewhere: 'Everything functions. What is uncanny is that it all functions and that this functioning pushes ahead to further functioning' (cited in Schurmann 1987: 41).
17. In the *Contributions* Heidegger writes: 'Yet how is the 'and' related to space, how to time? Has that ever been asked? Can it be asked at all?...The 'and' is in truth the ground of the essence of both space and time, the dislodging into the encompassing open realm which forms presencing and constancy but which could not itself be experienced or grounded' (Heidegger 2012: 296).
18. One can refer to Derrida's *Spectres of Marx* to see the full implications he draws out of the words 'the time is out of joint'.
19. This dislocation and disjuncture of Being as infinity of traces is what Derrida called *differance.*

References

Agamben, Giorgio, *Stanzas: Word and Phantasm in Western Culture,* trans. Ronald L. Martinez (Minneapolis: University of Minneapolis Press, 1993).

Aristotle, *Problems,* trans. W.S. Hett (Cambridge, Mass.: Harvard University Press, 1957).

Benjamin, Walter, *Selected Writings,* Vol. 2 Part 2, trans. Rodney Livingstone and others, eds. Michael W. Jennings, Howard Eiland and Gary Smith (London: Harvard University Press, 1999).

Burton, Robert, *The Anatomy of Melancholy: Being an Abridgement of Burton's Celebrated Work* (London: John Walker, 1824).

Butler, Judith, 'Melancholy Gender/Refused Identification' in *Psychoanalytic Dialogues,* Vol. 5, Iss. 2, 1995.

Derrida, Jacques, *Without Alibi,* trans. Peggy Kamuf (Stanford: Stanford University Press, 2002).

Derrida, Jacques, *The Work of Mourning,* ed. Pascale-Anne Braut and Michael Naas (Chicago: University of Chicago Press, 2001).

Derrida, Jacques, *Spurs: Nietzsche's Styles,* trans. Barbara Harlow (Chicago: University of Chicago Press, 1981).

Ferber, Ilit, *Philosophy and Melancholy: Benjamin's Early Reflections on Theater and Language* (Stanford: Stanford University Press, 2011).

Freud, Sigmund, 'Mourning and Melancholia' in *The Nature of Melancholy: From Aristotle to Kristeva,* ed. Jennifer Radden (Oxford: Oxford University Press, 2000).

Grossmith, Robert, 'The Book of Ands' in *The Book of Ands and Other Stories.* Kindle ed. (Big Lie Press, 2011).

Heidegger, Martin, *Being and Time,* trans. John Macquarrie and Edward Robinson (Oxford: Blackwell Publishers, 2001).

Heidegger, Martin, *Contributions to Philosophy (of the Event),* trans. Richard Rojcewicz and Daniela Vallega-Neu (Bloomington: Indiana University Press, 2012).

Heidegger, Martin, *Four Seminars,* trans. Andrew Mitchell and Francois Raffoul (Indiana: Indiana University Press, 2003).

Heidegger, Martin, *On Time and Being,* trans. Joan Stambaugh (New York: Harper Torchbooks, 1977).

Kant, Immanuel, *Anthropology from a Pragmatic Point of View,* trans. Victor Lyle Dowdell (Carbondale: Southern Illinois University Press, 1978).

Keats, John, 'Ode on Melancholy' in *The Poems of John Keats* ed. Edmund Blunden (New Delhi: Rupa Books, 2010).

Klibansky, Raymond, Erwin Panofsky and Saxl, Fritz, *Saturn and Melancholy* (London: Thomas Nelson and Sons, 1964).

Pinel, Phillipe, *A Treatise on Insanity: In Which are Contained the Principles of a New and More Practical Nosology of Maniacal* Disorders, trans. D.D. Davis (Sheffield: W. Todd Publishers, 1806).

Radden, Jennifer, *The Nature of Melancholy: From Aristotle to Kristeva* (Oxford: Oxford University Press, 2000).

Schürmann, Reiner, *Heidegger on Being and Acting: From Principles to Anarchy* (Bloomington: Indiana University Press, 1987).

Shakespeare, William, *As You Like It*, ed. Alan Brissenden (Oxford: Oxford University Press, 1993).

Shakespeare, William, *Hamlet*, ed. Cyrus Hoy (London: W.W. Norton, 1992).

Žižek, Slavoj, *Did Somebody Say Totalitarianism? Five Interventions in the (Mis) Use of a Notion* (London: Verso, 2001).

Žižek, Slavoj, *The Ticklish Subject: The Absent Centre of Political Ontology* (London: Verso, 1999).

Žižek, Slavoj, 'From Desire to Drive: Or Why Lacan is not a Lacanian' (*Žižek. livejournal.com/2226.html.*Web, 2004).

Aporetic Melancholies
Reading Paul Celan's Melancholy Poems

Sneha Chowdhury

Introduction

In his well-known speech 'The Meridian', delivered on the occasion of winning the George Buchner Prize in 1960, Paul Celan made a case for poetry, one that bears traces of Buchner's work. Celan variously defines poetry as an encounter, a breathturn (*Atemwende*), and something abyssal, all the while referring back to one intriguing character from Buchner's play *Danton's Death* called Lucille (Derrida 2005: 131). Celan argues that it is with Lucille's sudden, absurd cry, "Long Live the King!" that the poem in its unmixed solitude, in its singularity, is born (Ibid: 179).

Georges Danton had been one of the leaders of the French Revolution along with Robespierre. They were both part of the Revolutionary Government. As we all know, Robespierre was quite ruthless and had condemned many people to death. Danton had grown wary of Robespierre, and had started to have doubts about the Terror (the Reign of Terror) that had consigned opponents to the guillotine. Robespierre sensed this and immediately ordered the execution of Danton and his other allies, Camille and others. Lucille was Camille's wife. In the scene immediately following their execution, Lucille appears alone on stage. Her world has come to an end. She observes:

> Everything else is allowed to go on living…everything's astir, clocks tick, bells ring, folk pass, water flows, everything continues just as before, forever and ever—But no! It mustn't happen, no! I shall sit on the ground and scream, so everything stops, shocked into stillness, not a flicker of movement… . (Levine 2014: 38)

And then she screams, 'Long Live the King!' However, her cry has no impact on the audience. There is no silence. Instead, these words lead to her immediate arrest. These words, in fact, become her self-imposed death sentence. Her sudden cry betrays her ignorance to her husband's cause; it creates a rupture in their discourse: why else would she cry in favor of the King? Yet, her cry is also a cry of absolute empathy, of her spontaneous response to the event of death. Her cry is not interpretable, yet it bears meaning, a melancholic cry about her failure to express. Her cry is the promise of poetry; or, as Celan says, 'it is an act of freedom. It is a step' (Derrida 2005: 179).

Born Paul Antschel in Czernowitz, Romania, in 1920, Paul Celan's family was captured by German Nazi troops in 1941. In 1942, he learnt that his father had been killed in the labour camp, and later, his mother too had been shot by the Nazis. It is believed that his experience at Auschwitz and the death of his parents form the core of his poetry (Joris 1995: 14). But what we learn from his poetry is that the sayable is imbued with the unsayable: poetry bears the burden of the witness, who is also the survivor, having outlived those who succumbed to the trauma, those who couldn't live to speak their truth. In the aftermath of the trauma, poetry becomes an act of freedom, but also an act of responsibility; a gift to posterity by a witness who bears the burden of knowledge, knowledge granted by the privilege of life itself. One may, then, say that this paradox forms the core of Paul Celan's poetry. His experience and his ability to express are hinged on this paradox. This paradox takes on the character of an aporia, evident in Lucille's ironic cry, and is felt more sharply in his later poetry.

In his last collection of poems titled *Atemwende* (*Breathturn*) published in 1967, just three years before his death from suicide, one finds two poems on melancholy:

A.
Twenty forever
evaporated Keytower-flowers
in your swimming left
fist.
Into the fish-scale
etched:
the lines of the hand
which they outgrew.
Heaven- and earth acid
flowed together.
The time-reckoning
worked out, without remainder. Cruising:
—for your, quick melancholy, sake—
scale and fist. (Celan, 105)

B.
From fists, white
from the truth hammered
free of the wordwall,
a new brain blooms for you.
Beautiful, to be veiled by nothing,
it casts them, the
thought-shadows.
Therein, immovable,
fold up, even today,
twelve mountains, twelve foreheads.
The from you also star-eyed
loafer Melancholy
hears of it. (165)

But before we begin to understand or unpack how melancholy plays out in the poems, let us have a look at the history of the concept of melancholy.

A Brief History of Melancholy

It is, perhaps, very difficult to conclusively answer what melancholy means. As Ilit Ferber in 'The Idea of Melancholy' from *Philosophy and Melancholy* aptly notes, melancholy is what Walter Benjamin would call a 'worn-out word'; its history is fraught with diverse meanings and contradictions that do not lend themselves to an evolutionary development. Melancholy's history resembles the movement of a whirlpool (Ferber 2013: 3).

One of the earliest representations of melancholy, Albrecht Durer's 1514 engraving *Melencolia I*, depicts an angel sitting amidst what appears to be a dog, a cherub and sundry objects. The angel holds an object to write, but is disinterestedly looking away, bearing the burden of interpreting the world by herself. Across several interpretations of the painting, she stands as the quintessential symbol of melancholy. Similarly, one can also not forget John Keats' famous poem *Ode on Melancholy* composed in the year 1819 where the speaker urges the addressee to not give in to the things that cause melancholy—"...go not to Lethe, neither twist/Wolf's-bane, tight-rooted, for its poisonous wine". The speaker urges the addressee to *look away* and dwell on the 'morning rose', or on the beloved's eyes instead, turning melancholy into an enabling, productive emotion, from an incapacitating, disabling one: melancholy here becomes a mode of reflection and imagination.

If one further traces the history of melancholy, one notices that it has been variously described as a somatic condition (caused by excess black bile) resulting from the melancholic person's sins (in the Middle Ages); a mood (in the Renaissance); the result of "demonic" and evil pursuits (in the 17th century); as something that is desirable, providing impetus for work, hence the association with "genius" (in the nineteenth century); and finally, with Freud, as pathology (Ferber 2013: 2). Robert Burton rightly called it the 'many-headed beast' (quoted by Ferber 2013: 53).

What is more significant to note is that, despite this diversity in its conceptual framework, and in its history, all these different meanings are centered on the subjective state of the melancholic individual, that is, the subject generates the meaning of melancholy. This subjective bent is further consolidated in the Freudian concept of melancholy, as pathology: 'The strength of the psychoanalytic bent has transformed melancholy into a privileged private state, overshadowing the more far-reaching meanings the term encompasses' (Ibid: 2).

Ferber breaks through this heavy scaffolding of pathology in the discourse of melancholy, and re-thinks melancholy by focusing on the history of the concept itself, especially in the context of philosophy. David Hume for example, in his *A Treatise of Human Nature*, discourses on "philosophic melancholy", where he writes that melancholy is akin to philosophizing, or is the very condition for philosophizing because a philosopher needs to acknowledge the difference between "what is known" and "what is surmised". And in that acknowledgement, melancholy is born. Prior to Hume, John Locke categorizes melancholy as one of the seven symptoms of human misery. Locke defines melancholy as 'social withdrawal as "when it hinders discourse and conversation"'. Borrowing from Locke and further analyzing what Hume writes, one may conclude that a philosopher experiences "withdrawal" when he or she realizes the incommensurability between knowledge and the insufficiency of ideas in the pursuit of that knowledge. Melancholy, according to Hume, is inextricably linked to the pursuit of knowledge, or, to philosophy (Ingram 2011: 70-71).

From the premise given above, one may begin to think that, due to its relationship with philosophy, melancholy is also related to truth. One may also add that, through its relationship with truth, we begin to see that the subjective weight of melancholy is relieved, as will also be demonstrated in the subsequent paragraphs. Ferber rightly asks: 'If truth is not internal or subjective but the subject matter of philosophical activity itself, how do we reconcile philosophy with melancholic closure and self-absorption?' (Ferber 2011: 54).

In "Leibniz's Monad", this contradiction is taken up by looking at a monad's relationship with the world. Very interestingly, through her study of the history of the concept of melancholy and Leibniz's monad, Ferber concludes that this paradoxical or contradictory nature of melancholy is ontological. She thereby attributes the monad's relationship with the world to this "structure" of melancholy.

One might do well to mention that Ferber's formulation of the ontology of "philosophical melancholy" or, the melancholy structure is heavily mediated by Heidegger's formulation of "mood" in *Being and Time*: 'The implications of exploring such co-existence reach beyond the understanding of melancholy's special relationship to philosophy: They divulge the essential bond between philosophy and mood (or attunement) in general' (Ferber 2011: 54).

According to Heidegger, the history of philosophy is a lesson in forgetting a crucial question, that is, the question concerning Being. The question concerning Being is forgotten for several reasons—it is universal, it is undefinable, it's a concept; and different entities, different beings are already subsumed under it. The ontico-ontological analysis of being will only be possible if one is first open to the question of Being. This openness is guided by a certain *Stimmung*, which is German word for one's mood or attunement to the question of Being. It is this mood or attunement that de-structures the history of philosophy (or, the history of knowledge-production) that has covered up the question concerning Being. The affective putting forth of the being that is open to the question of Being is called *Dasein*. It is this affect or mood that guides the *thrownness* of existence into the world with others where it is always-already ex-centric and makes a proper existential analysis of Dasein possible.

The *subjective* import of melancholy is also thoroughly broken down in Leibniz's concept of the monad. A monad "expresses" its relationship with the world through a kind of "radical interiority". Monad is a closed structure, and it has no existence with the world outside the contours of its "being". When one says that the monad "expresses" its relationship with the world, one must remember that this is not a subjective expression of intentionality. Ferber notes that this expression is *attuned* to the world, and that this attunement is a manifestation of a certain *mood*. This attunement is *affective* but *non-subjective*. This will perhaps become clearer with the following excerpt from Leibniz:

> So we also sense some confused result of all the motions taking place within us, but, being accustomed to this internal motion, we do not perceive it clearly and with reflection except when there is an important change as in the *beginning of illness.* (Ferber 2011: 61)

From the aforementioned excerpt one may deduce that something changes when one falls ill, or when one experiences pain. The pain is exceptional and, in pain, a monad expresses its relationship with the world. At this juncture one must clarify that this is not similar to the pain and melancholy experienced by Freud's melancholic in *Mourning and Melancholy*. One may recall that Freud's melancholic is a *subject* who suffers an *object-cathexis*. There is a causal relationship between the melancholic subject and the object loss. Melancholy is conditioned by the *present-absence* of the object. But, for the monad, there is no causal relationship between itself and the world. The world is *felt* through its pain. The expression of the world is subsumed under its radical interiority (Ibid: 61).

Both Leibniz and Heidegger, separately, teach us that it is possible to connect with the world in a way that does not require the subject to treat the world as an object of knowledge with a set of attributes rendered *graspable* or interpretable through pre-given ideas. Both teach us that pain and *angst*, respectively, are necessary affects for forsaking our subjectivities, not to strengthen our subjectivities by reflecting on the successful or failed pursuit of knowledge about the world as an object. This is a necessary understanding for our reading of melancholy in Celan's poems. But our reading of melancholy in Paul Celan's poems also necessitates an understanding of the concept of melancholy deployed by Walter Benjamin in *The Origin of German Tragic Drama* to begin our departure from the subjective grounding of melancholy. In fact, any discussion of melancholy remains incomplete without looking at Benjamin's discussion of the melancholy allegory of the Baroque explored in this text.

In the 'Epistemo-Critical Prologue' to this text, Benjamin undertakes a detailed analysis of his method for the text. Benjamin argues that there is no one way street between truth and knowledge and therefore, melancholy, which has been so far seen as the first condition or the result of this journey, has to be thought anew. Benjamin corrects the positivistic notion of truth by arguing that truth is not something that can be possessed through the accumulation of knowledge, or that, truth is not the *presentation* of knowledge; knowledge here being the mere acquiring of phenomena or objects. On the other hand, truth is "unpossessable" and is impossible to present; truth can only be *represented*. This is his premise for further explaining the difference between *Trauerspiel* and classical tragedy in the text. Truth, here, is not the Aristotelian notion of truth as the adequate (*adequatio*) agreement between the sign and the signifier, but truth as transcendental: transcendental but immanent in the mode of representation, that is, immanent in the form. Truth is form. But this is not adequately given in classical tragedy which heavily relies on mythology, which act as referents for the overriding moral structure of the plays and create symbols of good and evil. Benjamin argues that this is given in the allegorical structure of the *Trauerspiel* (Cowan 1981: 111).

Allegory divests itself of symbolism and becomes a historical form in which truth is represented. As critic Bainard Cowan adroitly notes: 'The affirmation of the existence of truth, then, is the first precondition for allegory; the second is the recognition of its *absence*' (Ibid: 114). When Cowan writes about truth in this mode, he means that truth is transcendental. In classical tragedy, this would be the moment towards the end of the play, the climax, when any element in the play aims towards its resolution; this is the moment when everything begins to *make sense*. Truth, in the *Trauerspiel*, is not dialectically represented; truth is not teleological. But truth in the allegorical sense, is eschatological; truth is hinged to something that is imminent, about to come, never entirely assimilable to the *meaningful* language of the tragedy. The melancholic hero of the *Trauerspiel* is afflicted with a melancholy that is neither the cause, nor the result of anything. His melancholy is inassimilable. In *Danton's Death*, Lucille's cry is the tragic cry of, and for justice. Functioning as the *deus ex machina* in the play, her cry suddenly stops the play in its tracks. What could 'Long Live the King!' really mean in the context of the play? Her cry is ironic—it betrays her husband's "cause", and is absurd to the monarchy. Lucille's melancholy is inassimilable to the language of the play, to its meaning. Lucille's cry is poetry.

Melancholy in Celan's Poems

Now let's tread upon the path opened up by Benjamin and arrive at Paul Celan's poems. One of the distinct characteristics of the first poem in the series is that the language of the poem is temporalised. The poem opens with a fixed time—twenty forever. The two other fixed and static elements in the poem are the "swimming fist" and the "fish-scale". But despite these fixed elements, the poem also shows the belatedness of time. One may say that the poem is belated; the poem has not arrived in time to see the flower, the fish and the hand that held the fish. The poem accounts for the passage of time—"time-reckoning worked out"—but the passage of time has only brought loss. It is important to note that time is in a double bind here. Those which ought to have been *reckoned* with time—the objects that a melancholic dwells on—are absent. What are left are traces of the objects, no "remainders". For "melancholy's sake" we see only a fist and a scale, words reminiscent of what is amiss. In the second poem, thinking is set free from the "wordwall" of language. The brain released from the fist casts "thought-shadows", not thoughts. Truth, here, is neither assimilable to language, nor to thoughts. The thought-shadows carry with them "mountains" and "foreheads". Melancholy, personalised as a loafer, is drawn towards them.

At this juncture, it would be useful to recall Husserl's notion of time *vis-à-vis* knowledge. Husserl talks about two knowledge types. Type one is metaphysical knowledge or a knowledge that emerges from inadequate givenness of things (*a priori* knowledge, hence fixed and transcendental); and type two is the knowledge that emerges from things which are immanent, that is, things which are adequately given. This adequate givenness is always gauged and constituted over time through intentionality. The continuous correspondence between the knower and the thing to be known through their intention to transform inadequate givenness to adequate givenness is phenomenology, according to Husserl. In this correspondence, the subject is constituted in its intentionality over linear time (Husserl 1999: 4). This intentionality is denied in the first poem. What remains are traces and not the things themselves, indicating that the things amiss are not assimilable to melancholy, and melancholy inassimilable to them.

On a similar note, the second poem sheds light on the inadequacy of thought by replacing it with its shadow, its trace. While Heidegger would find a way for thought through the word because of his hope for a meta-language that cannot be contained in names which accord mere attributes to things[1], the poem dismisses such a "wordwall" and sets its truth free all the while acknowledging the double-bind of language which fails one but which also compels one to express. Such double-binds and aporias form the core of Celan's poetry. In *Aporias*, Jacques Derrida writes,

> Of the *aporos* or of the *aporia*: the difficult or the impracticable, here the impossible, passage, the refused, denied, or prohibited passage, indeed the nonpassage, which can in fact be something else, the event of a coming or of a future advent... no longer has the form of the movement that consists in passing, traversing, or transiting. It would be the "coming to pass" of an event that would no longer have the form or the appearance of a *pas*: in sum, a coming without *pas*. (Derrida 1995: 8)

Derrida argues that all truth claims are finite and confined, rather limited, its contours compel us to overstep them, betray the truth and make different claims all the while being aware of the (im) possible task ahead of us. Aporia plays out in the poems in the way melancholy marks a lack of referents, but not a total lack. Melancholy is aporetic because it does not become the guiding affect to constitute one's subjectivity. In fact, the poems critique intentionality and subjective knowledge. Celan's poems, like Lucille's tragic melancholic cry, stand at the threshold of experience, *expressing* the burden of experience that escapes language.

Notes

1. Can one forget Stefan George's memorable poem *The Word* and Heidegger's reading of the poem in *The Nature of Language*?:

   The Word
   Wonders from dreams and from abroad
   I carried to my country's port,

   But for the names I had to wait
   Which in her depths were searched by Fate.

   Then I could hold them in my hand
   And now they blossom in this land ...

   Once I returned from such a tour
   With a small treasure rich and pure;

   She searched for long but had to tell
   That no such thing slept in her well;

   At once it vanished from my hand
   And ne'er this wealth entered the land ...

   So, sadly, I became aware
   That things are not if words aren't there.

References

Benjamin, Walter, *The Origin of German Tragic Drama*, trans. John Osborne (London:Verso, 2009).

Celan, Paul, *Breathturn* (Los Angeles: Sun & Moon, 1995).

Cowan, Bainard, 'Walter Benjamin's Theory of Allegory' in *New German Critique* (1981), no. 22, 109-122. Accessed: 09-10-2017.

Derrida, Jacques, *Aporias,* trans. Thomas Dutoit (Stanford: Stanford University Press, 1995).

Derrida, Jacques, 'The Meridian by Paul Celan' in *Sovereignties in Question: The Poetics of Paul Celan*, trans. Thomas Dutoit, and Outi Pasanen (New York: Fordham University Press, 2005), 173-186.

Ferber, Ilit, 'Leibniz's Monad: A Study in Melancholy and Harmony' in *Philosophy's Moods: The Affective Grounds of Thinking*, edited by Hagi Kenaan and Ilit Ferber (Springer, 2011), 53-68.

Ferber, Ilit, *Philosophy and Melancholy: Benjamin's Early Reflections on Theater and Language* (Stanford: Stanford University Press, 2013).

Heidegger, Martin, 'The Nature of Language' in *On the Way to Language*, trans. Peter D. Hertz (New York: Harper & Row, 1971), 57-110.

Husserl, Edmund, *The Idea of Phenomenology*, trans. Lee Hardy (Springer, 1999).

Ingram, Allan, et al, *Melancholy Experience in Literature of the Long Eighteenth Century Before Depression, 1660-1800* (Palgrave Macmillan, 2011).

Joris, Pierre, 'Introduction' in *Breathturn*, trans. Pierre Joris (Los Angeles: Sun & Moon, 1995), 13-51.

Keats, John, "Ode on Melancholy", *Poetry Foundation*, https://www.poetryfoundation.org/poems/44478/ode-on-melancholy

Levine, Michael G, 'Pendant: Celan, Buchner, and the Terrible Voice of the Meridian' in *A Weak Messianic Power: Figures of a Time to Come in Benjamin, Derrida, and Celan* (New York: Fordham University Press, 2014), 37-62.

'Living Leaves Traces'
Looking at Melancholy Through Sculptures

Swarnika Ahuja

> Just think how many thoughts a blanket smothers while one lies alone in bed, and how many unhappy dreams it keeps warm.
>
> —Franz Kafka

The idea of melancholy and melancholic writing on and through objects is not a completely new one, be it in poetry, painting, sculpture or art. Rather, objects have often acquired a reflective nature, have been visualised as a mode of melancholic contemplation in poetry and art. Keats in 'Ode on a Grecian Urn' poetises this notion of pleasure and loss as he sings in a celebratory tone,

> Heard melodies are sweet, but those unheard
> Are sweeter; therefore, ye soft pipes, play on;
> Not to the sensual ear, but, more endear'd,
> Pipe to the spirit ditties of no tone:
> Fair youth, beneath the trees, thou canst not leave
> Thy song, nor ever can those trees be bare;
> Bold Lover, never, never canst thou kiss,
> Though winning near the goal—yet, do not grieve;
> She cannot fade, though thou hast not thy bliss,
> For ever wilt thou love, and she be fair! (Keats 2009: 238)

An old relic of the Antiquity invigorates a kind of happiness in him, as he realises that 'the bold lover never, never canst kiss'. This notion of partaking of pleasure of what one cannot have becomes central not only to this poem but to the idea of melancholy and loss itself: It is the unheard, one that has been lost, that becomes all the more sweeter. In a sense, Keats' poem makes the Grecian Urn itself the object through which he can then ruminate the loss of time itself, the loss of an age of philosophical greatness that now remains only as traces through these relics of art, of sculpture in the world of objects. But even in this loss he finds happiness, for he bestows immortality, like the ones bestowed to the lovers in the urn itself, to this object that stands to symbolise the loss of the greatness of an age gone by. Through this sculptural remnant he combines emotions of loss and pleasure; he chooses not to grieve but memorialise and 'museumise' art and take joy in that loss, in unheard melodies.

In this essay I would like to argue that certain objects of art, of sculpture become crucial to contemplate the anatomy of loss itself, archiving traces and impressions of a lost time infused with a certain kind mood that is melancholic. Often in the works of Giorgio, sculpture or specifically statues appear to evoke a sense of desolation, emptiness and melancholia. By placing statues in the style of classical art in secluded and open surreal streets and spaces, he evokes a mood that is deeply melancholic. Juxtaposed between the modern and the classical, sculptures in his art appear as if abandoned and forgotten, displaced as if occupying the realm of memory itself.

To quote from www.theartstory.com

> Key to Giorgio de Chirico's work is his love of the classical past. He came to this through his appreciation for German Romanticism, and it was this that revealed to him new ways of looking at the Classics, and ways of treating themes of tragedy, enigma, and melancholy. For de Chirico, the themes and motifs of the Greek and Roman Classics remained valid even in the modern world. However, he recognized that the clash of the past and present produced strange effects—suggesting sorrow, disorientation, nostalgia—and some of the most powerful qualities in his work of the 1910s come from staging this contrast.

de Chirico, Giorgio. *The Song of Love* c. 1914

Interestingly, Ida Tomshinsky in *Gloves: History and Present* notes that this 'original painting brings together incongruous and unrelated objects: the head of a classical Greek statue, an oversized rubber glove, a green ball, and a train shrouded in darkness, silhouetted against a bright blue sky...Cloaked in an atmosphere of anxiety and melancholy, de Chirico's humanoid forms, vacuous architecture, shadowy passages and inharmoniously elongated streets evoke the profound absurdity of a universe torn apart by World War 1.' (Tomshinsky 2011: 56).

de Chirico, Giorgio. *Mystery and Melancholy of a Street.* c. 1914

It almost appears that he uses space and light in such a way that his paintings draw out a sense of abandonment. There is an attempt to clutter the canvas with things, objects, and sculptures almost to evoke the futility of these symbols of high art in a world reduced to meaninglessness by war.

Similarly, he employs absolute vacant spaces to create a mood expressive of deep loss and mourning. Placing a statue or a half-formed hint of a half-made sculpture in large uninhibited spaces ultimately becomes a metaphor for profound apathy. Giorgio de Chirico's melancholic mood in this differs from Keats' sense of celebration that is unified and consoled by the high ideals of Beauty and Truth that survive in the stead of the great classical age.

de Chirico, Giorgio. *The Uncertainty of the Poet.* c. 1913

Fragmented and torn asunder by a post-war experience, de Chirico's use of sculpture, of pottery, of objects all thrown together with everyday objects in a frame create a sense of tragic loss. The canvas itself breaks up into parts into these objects creating a jarring effect when viewed together. Like the consciousness of a person. What the solitariness of the statue achieves either by standing forgotten in the shadow of a street or by lying confused in a heap, like trash, like garbage, thrown away disrespectfully rather than showcased prominently is to symbolize a deep sense of loss that is tragic because these objects acquire a sense of obscurity in his art. They seem to mourn the loss of not only an age of greatness but also the impossibility of the recovery of those unified Ideals of Truth and Beauty.

de Chirico, Giorgio. *The Melancholy of Departure.* c. 1914

Here is an entry from www. visual-arts-cork.com:

> The purpose of the many allusions to the classical world in de Chirico's paintings of the period was *not* to illustrate aspects of the past but to act as tokens or symbols of the imagination and memory. He began painting scenes of Italian piazzas suffused in warm Mediterranean sunshine only after his arrival in Paris in 1911, and thus, in a sense, this whole series of works was based on fantasy rather than direct experience. It was characteristic of his ambiguous approach to the classical world that the torso in *The Uncertainty of the Poet* was probably a modern plaster cast based on an original piece of Greek or Roman sculpture. The sense of the torso being several times removed from the original is heightened by the anti-naturalist manner in which it is painted: the black outline and areas of crude hatching deliberately recall the style of academic figure drawing and engraving. In fact de Chirico often took his images of classical statues from illustrations in manuals and textbooks, and in so doing emphasized the unreality of his images. In this way his paintings suggested that the past was irretrievably lost and could only be replaced by copies and pastiches.

de Chirico, Giorgio. *The Enigma of the Hour.* c. 1911

With its starkly receding perspective, deep shadows and the regular pattern of the arcade, this painting is dominated by line and geometric shapes. De Chirico believed that great art was based not on copying nature but, as he wrote at the time, on "dimensions, lines, and forms of eternity and the infinite"; and these, he claimed, were present above all in Greek and Roman architecture. What he valued in classical colonnades and piazzas was not so much their order and rationality as their strange lyrical beauty.'

The Enigma of the Hour and *Mystery* and *Melancholy of a Street* especially become mediative mood-pieces that ponder upon what has been left behind. The loneliness of the statues in unreal dream-like scapes use shade, color and shadows to express a vastness that is despairing; they are pregnant with the possibility of a revelation that is imminent, a mystery whose resolution haunts the painting. It is suffused with the possibility of making meaning, of saying something that is on the tip of one's tongue dangerously close to complete understanding of what that great truth is, but is still evaded, deferred and ultimately lost, leaving behind only the traces of what that final solution was.

What sculptures and objects do in Chirico's paintings is that they appear like missing pieces of a jigsaw puzzle, like essential parts of a larger project of meaning–making, of the very mystery of existence and their sense of displacement and abandonment which gesture towards the absolute loneliness of the human subject in a vast and apathetic universe .

Therefore, the use of the Roman arcade becomes a recurring trope in his art to deepen this sense of obsoleteness, obscurity and abandonment culminating into a mood of melancholy. In *The Enigma of the Hour,* the regularity with which the Roman arcade is depicted evokes an uncertainty of time. The clock is transfixed, and stands as a symbol of modern technologies of measuring time, articulating the rise of industrial time against which the deeply resonant shadow cast by the old architectural arcade is juxtaposed. In the face of the certainty of clock time, the use of the Roman arcade evokes a sense of time that is less certain, more ambiguous, and therefore, more enigmatic and haunting. This pronounced contrast reduces the Roman arcade as a representing a tradition of recording time, the position of the Sun and shadows that will never return, or, at least will never find any useful existence in the age of industrial clock time. This renders the notion of enigma very closely to that of melancholy.

This deep sense of mystery that arises as a consequence of this juxtaposition is never easily reconciled. And Chirico does not want it to be reconciled either. He rather wants to focus on this enigma of the past in the present that invariably haunts the painting. In trying to capture the slow percolation of history in the everyday that takes place almost anonymously, he renders the whole edifice eerie which is melancholic precisely because of this paradox at the heart of modern existence. The clock occupies only a tiny space in the painting and yet no matter how much it appears to be out of joint in this classical architectural setting, the central presence of the modern clock renders the past as only illusory.

Our gaze tries to resolve this paradox, because at the heart of it what has truly been painted is not a simple imitation of the old architectural styles even though that is what it appears to be the subject of the painting but rather the apparition of the past, the past that can only be an apparition in the present. This is not to deny that the past does not have a material existence but due to its unsuccessful reconciliation with the present, it will exist in the present as always already abandoned, out of joint, as only a jigsaw piece, as a relic, uprooted from its own time and space, that will never be retrieved, and be felt by a certain people located in a different and specific place and time.

> There is nothing like the enigma of the Arcade which the Romans invented. A street, an arch: the sun looks different when it bathes a Roman wall in light. And there is something about it more mysteriously plaintive than in French architecture, and less ferocious too. The Roman Arcade is a fatality. Its voice speaks in riddles filled with a strangely Roman poetry, of shadows on old walls and a curious music. (Giorgio de Chirico "Manuscript from the Collection of the Late Paul Eluard 1911-1915 as cited in Soby, *Giorgio de Chirico:* 247)

From an entry from www. visual-arts-cork.com:

> During his studies in Munich, de Chirico had admired Otto Weininger's writings on the philosophy of geometrical shapes; and in an article in *Valori Plastici* of 1919 he quoted Weininger's view that the arc, unlike the circle, is incomplete and fosters a sense of uncertainty and expectation. As this suggests, de Chirico's obsession with line and geometry in his compositions in this period was not mathematical: the raking perspectives and receding arcades were for him the pictorial equivalents of a projection of the consciousness or such emotional states as anticipation and nostalgia.

The melancholia of this complete incompleteness of shape, form and object becomes reminiscent of the fragmentation of a person's selfhood. In Chirico's case, the war brings out this realisation of the profound loss of pieces of the self, of what is missing and will continue to remain missing. In a great sense what has been tossed away with these great sculptural works is the belief and faith in salvation of man through art itself. And this is precisely what de Chirico's works mourn. Like Camus's articulation of the myth of Sisyphus, they oscillate between a seesaw of emotions-of hope and despair. Like that moment when Sisyphus is about to reach the top of the mountain and is inches away from his salvation before the rock slips from his grip once again.

Thus, the deep sense of eeriness, of mystery that, statues and nameless streets conjure all become clues to a mystery that can never be solved. They evoke a deep sense of melancholia due to a complex intermingling of pleasure caused by the excitement of trying to solve this great mystery and angst at the same time that is based on the realisation of the futility to do so. The deep sense of emptiness draws the eye of the spectator deeper and deeper. The impossibility of knowing what lies at the other end of this mystery never makes us tear away from the frame but pulls us further and further intensifying the experience of looking at the art object for us.

Kafka, Franz. *The Thinker*. c. 1913

Kafka, Franz. *Fencing. c.* 1917

Kafka, Franz. *Three Runners.* c. 1912-1913

Giorgio de Chirico's works are rendered a Kafkaesque quality. For like 'in Kafka these two worlds are that of everyday life on the one hand, and, on the other, that of supernatural anxiety. It seems that we are witnessing here an interminable exploitation of Nietzsche's remark: 'Great problems are in the street.' (Camus 2013: 80)

Giacometti, Alberto. *The Walking Man.* c. 1961

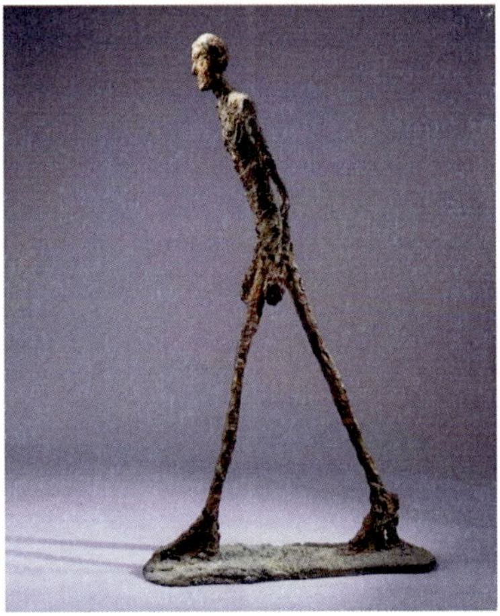

Giacometti, Alberto. *Man Pointing.* c. 1947

And this great sense of mystery lingers in the sculptures of Alberto Giacometti. In a sense they look like 3D models of Kafka's two-dimensional sketches, in so far as they try to capture the thin stick-like figures gesturing towards something- never ever performing an act completely but always in the process of it.

> In the years leading up to World War II, Giacometti abandoned his earlier Surrealism. Dissatisfied with the resource of imagination, he returned to the resource of vision, focusing on the human figure and working from live models. Under his eyes, however, these models seem virtually to have dissolved. Working in clay (the preparation to casting in bronze), Giacometti scraped away the body's musculature, so that the flesh seems eaten off by a terrible surrounding emptiness, or to register the air around it as a hostile pressure. Recording the touch of the artist's fingers, the surface of *Man Pointing* is as rough as if charred or corroded. At the same time, the figure dominates its space, even from a distance. (excerpt from The Museum of Modern Art, *MoMA Highlights*, New York: The Museum of Modern Art, revised 2004, originally published 1999: 214)

Giacometti manipulated distance very carefully in his sculptures. Unlike the cluttering of classical motifs on Chirico, the sculptures of Giacometti are closer in appearance to Kafka's art, stick-thin figure, reduced to their bare bones standing absolutely alone in a vast undefined space that surrounds them.

Giacometti, Alberto. *City Square.* c. 1948

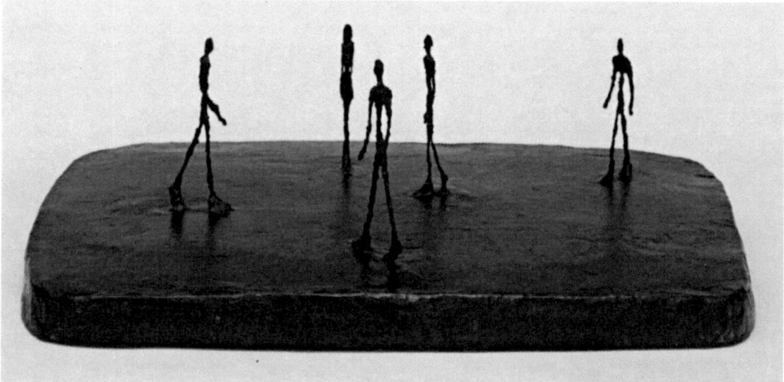

Jean Paul Sartre wrote explicitly about Giacommeti's sculptures in *Essays in Aesthetics* (1963). He describes the necessity of this so-called distance created by Giacometti. While the approach is different, it is in a sense similar to the sense of mystery and eeriness in Chirico's art:

> His figurines are solitary, but when placed together, no matter how, they are united by their solitude and transformed into a small magical society. (Sartre 1963: 48)

Possibly commenting on his *City Square*, he further writes:

Giacometti, Alberto. *Walking in the Rain.* c. 1948

> One of Giacometti's scenes is a crowd. He has sculptured men crossing a public square without seeing each other; they pass, hopelessly alone and yet together; they will be forever lost from each other, yet would never lose each other if they had not sought each other. He defined his universe better than I possibly could when he wrote, concerning one of his groups, that it reminded him of a part of a forest observed during the course of many years . . . a forest in which trees with barren, slender trunks seemed like people who had stopped in their tracks and were speaking to each other. [...] Giacometti became a sculptor because of his obsession with emptiness. About one statuette he wrote: "Me, rushing down a street in the rain." (Ibid: 48-49)

Reminiscent of what Camus wrote on Kafka quoting Nietzsche that incidentally rings true for Chirico as well, for Giacometti too: 'Great Problems are in the streets'. But his sculptures don't confound us with the bewildering cluttered emptiness of Chirico's works. Rather he manipulates the always already present space and throws his sculptures in that void.

And this is what Sartre expresses:

> But imagine a lyrical sculptor: what he tries to reproduce is his inner feeling, the boundless vacuum that surrounds him, leaving him defenceless and exposing him to the storm. Giacometti is a sculptor because he wears his vacuum as a snail its shell, because he wants to explain all its facets and dimensions [...] By kneading plaster, he creates a vacuum from a plenum. The figure when it leaves his fingers is "ten steps away, " and no matter what we do, it remains there. The statue itself determines the distance from which it must be viewed. [...] The situation engenders the surrounding no man's land. Each of his figures is Giacometti himself producing his little local vacuum. Yet all these slight absences that are as much a part of us as our names, as our shadows, are not enough to make a world. There is also the Void, the universal distance between all things. The street is empty, drinking in the sun; suddenly, in this empty space a human being appears. (Ibid: 49-50)

Giacometti, Alberto. *Diego.* c. 1964

Writing specifically on Giacometti's *Diego*, Sartre tries to look at how it flickers between presence and absence, between being and nothingness.

> How can one paint a vacuum? Before Giacometti it seems that no one had made the attempt. For five hundred years painters had been filling their canvases to the bursting point, forcing into them the whole universe. Giacometti begins by expelling the world from his canvases. For example, he paints his brother Diego all alone, lost in a hangar, and that is sufficient. [...] He is there, the wall is there, that is all. Nothing encloses him, nothing supports him, nothing contains him; he appears all alone within the vast frame of empty space. With each of his paintings Giacometti takes us back to the moment of creation ex nihilo.
>
> Each painting restates the old meta-physical question:
>
> Why is there something rather than nothing? And yet there is something: this stubborn, unjustifiable, superfluous apparition. The painted person is hallucinatory because presented in the form of an interrogative apparition.
>
> And yet Giacometti wants to paint what he sees just as he sees it. He wants the figures at the heart of their original vacuum on his motionless canvas forever to fluctuate between continuity and discontinuity. [...] At the same time, however, we cannot look at the canvas without uneasiness. We have an irrepressible urge to call for a flashlight or at least a candle. Is it a haze, the fading light of day, or our tired eyes? [...] When I discover a face in the fire, for example, or in an inkblot, or in the design of a curtain, the shape that has abruptly appeared becomes rigid and forces itself upon me. Even though I can see it in no other way than this, I know that others will see it differently. But the face in the fire has no truth while in Giacometti's paintings we are provoked and at the same time bewitched by the fact that there is a truth and that we are certain of it. It is there, right under my nose, whether I look for it or not. But my vision blurs, my eyes tire, I give up. Then I begin to understand that Giacometti overpowers us because he has reversed the facts in stating the problem. [...] And nothing prevents me from continuing to turn, obsessed by the phantom face that is constantly being formed, deformed and reformed behind me. The remarkable

> part is its credibility. Hallucinations also make their appearance on the periphery only to disappear when viewed directly. [...] But their reappearance is marked by a violent affirmation. They are like muffled shouts rising to the top of a mountain and informing the hearer that somewhere someone is grieving or calling for help. The alternation of appearance and disappearance, of flight and provocation, lends to Giacometti's figures a certain air of coquetry. [...] Coquettish, yes, and graceful because they are pure action, and sinister because of the emptiness that surrounds them, these creatures of nothingness achieve a plenum of existence by eluding and mystifying us[...]In spite of his knowledge, however, he has not lost hope. One day he will show us a portrait of Diego just like all others in appearance.
>
> We shall be forewarned and know that it is but a phantom, a vain illusion, a prisoner in its frame. And yet on that day, before the mute canvas we shall feel a shock, a very small shock. The very same shock that we feel on returning late and seeing a stranger walking toward us in the dark. (Ibid:. 51-59)

What makes their art subtly associated with melancholy is that they evoke this sense of incompleteness. They strike us as a heap of fragments of meaning, archiving only a mood of loss in the stead of the last piece of tile that completes the mosaic. Their art grows like a collection of things carved out of debris, of trash itself, representing broken parts. Out of a profound sense of wonderment we will chase the missing shards of meaning like a detective, rendering the spectator as a melancholic figure who sifts through the trash of history only to be eluded, only to encounter loss. Like Keats' lovers no moment in time will capture the pleasure of complete consummation but only leave the melancholia of a wasteland behind for us.

References

Keats, John, "Ode on a Grecian Urn", in *Complete Poems and Selected Letters of John Keats*, ed. with an Introduction by Edward Hirsch (Random House Publishing Group, 2009), 238.

Camus, Albert, "Appendix: Hope and the Absurd in the Work of Franz Kafka" in *The Myth of Sisyphus and Other Essays*, ed. with an Afterword by James Wood, trans. Justin O' Brien (United Kingdom: Penguin, 2013) p. 80.

Giorgio de Chirico "Manuscript from the Collection of the Late Paul Eluard 1911-1915 as cited in Soby, *Giorgio de Chirico,* p. 247.

"Giorgio De Chirico, Artist Overview and Analysis". [Internet]. 2017. TheArtStory.org Content compiled and written by The Art Story Contributors, Edited and published by The Art Story Contributors Available from: http://www.theartstory.org/artist-de-chirico-giorgio.htm [Accessed 1 Sep 2017].

Sartre, Jean-Paul, "The Paintings of Giacometti" in *Essays in Aesthetics* (1963), ed., selected and trans. by Wade Baskin (New York: Philosophical Library Inc., 1963) pp. 48-59.

The Museum of Modern Art, *MoMA Highlights*, New York: The Museum of Modern Art, revised 2004, originally published 1999, p. 214) [Accessed 1 Sep 2017].

"The Uncertainty of the Poet (1913)." *Uncertainty of the Poet, Giorgio de Chirico: Analysis*, www.visual-arts-cork.com/paintings-analysis/uncertainty-of-the-poet.htm. [Accessed 1 Sep 2017].

Tomshinsky, Ida, "Gloves in Fine Arts: Museum Collections and Displays" in *Gloves: History and Present* (Xlibris Corporation: 2011), p. 56.

List of Paintings

Chirico, Giorgio de. *The Song of Love.* 1914, Tate Modern, London, United Kingdom

Chirico, Giorgio de. *Mystery and Melancholy of a Street.* 1914, Tate Modern, London, United Kingdom

Chirico, Giorgio de. *The Melancholy of Departure.* 1914, Tate Modern, London, United Kingdom

Chirico, Giorgio de. *The Uncertainty of the Poet.* 1913, Tate Modern, London, United Kingdom.

Chirico, Giorgio de. *The Enigma of the Hour.* 1911, Tate Modern, London, United Kingdom.

Kafka, Franz. *The Thinker.* 1913. *http://www.openculture.com/2014/02/the-art-of-franz-kafka-drawings-from-1907-1917.html.* 1 Sep 2017.

Kafka, Franz. *Fencing.* 1917. *http://www.openculture.com/2014/02/the-art-of-franz-kafka-drawings-from-1907-1917.html.* 1 Sep 2017.

Kafka, Franz. *Three Runners.* 1912-1913. *http://www.openculture.com/2014/02/the-art-of-franz-kafka-drawings-from-1907-1917.html.* 1 Sep 2017.

Giacometti, Alberto. *The Walking Man*. 1961, MoMA, New York City, New York, USA.

Giacometti, Alberto. *Man Pointing*. 1947, MoMA, New York City, New York, USA.

Giacometti, Alberto. *City Square*. 1948, MoMA, New York City, New York, USA.

Giacometti, Alberto. *Walking in the Rain*. 1948, MoMA, New York City, New York, USA.

Giacometti, Alberto. *Diego*. 1964, MoMA, New York City, New York, USA.

Domains of Private Melancholy
The Burden of Language

Priyanka Das

The philosophical debate over language and its agency in acquisition of knowledge and in constructing behavioral patterns has a conspicuous history. It is therefore striking to note that insignificant effort is attempted to explore the undeviating and unwavering nexus between language and melancholy. It triggers certain palpable questions of how attainment of linguistic command determines the psychological disposition of an individual, and what role, if any, does the socio-political hegemonic institutional structures play in inducing chaos and melancholy in the subject. The subject matter of this paper may well be conceived as an elementary affair, demanding no doubt a good deal of perusal, an awareness of the historical context, and application of that knowledge, the rethinking of semantic or behavioral patterns in context to melancholy within linguistically dejected individuals or community as a whole.

Language is the one thing vital for our existence which makes us a subject worthy of social interaction. As such, language constitutes a parameter of contestation at every level of our social existence. Even the mere act of thinking takes place through the medium of language. Yet many of us perceive it challenging and onerous to pick up a new tongue. The dichotomy has been given due recognition by several theorists and linguists who have speculated semantic and lexical properties of language which would enable further researchers to draw a connection between language and melancholy.

Going back to the roots of language debate, as early as the beginning of the Western philosophical thought, one might find it pertinent to correlate 'Plato's problem'[1] with modern linguistic discourse. Advocating the agency of nature in opposition to nurture, Plato believed in the innate nature of language. Centuries later, Descartes championed this theory in his own line by recognizing the ability to learn and make use of language as the indispensable attribute of distinguishing an individual from machines or beasts, pronouncing how the stupidest person can learn a language while the smartest beast cannot (Descartes 1637/1988). This belief in the rationality of the human soul later influenced Noam Chomsky to dig into the creativity involved in the everyday utterance of human beings and in devising universal principles behind every language. Locke proposed an anti-thesis of *tabula rasa* or conceptualizing the brain as a blank slate which gains experience only through sensory perception, thus negating the innate nature of cognizance (Locke 1994: 311). Later B.F. Skinner, a behavioral scientist, expanded this theory by stressing more on the cognizance through the brain's response to external stimuli, thus rejecting the innate programming of the human brain. He went into details to show how language learning is cultivated through a rigorous process of reinforcement and punishment, which he terms as 'operant conditioning' whereby an individual is conditioned into saying the right things (Skinner 1938). This nurturing of language is a part of a continuous feedback where the society's reaction to an individual will largely depend on his speech. The last word on this regard was propounded by the nonpareil linguist Noam Chomsky who laid out the principle of Universal Grammar and gifted human brain with LAD (Language Acquisition Device) which contests Skinner's theory and foregrounds the innateness of cognizance. This roughly solves the dubiety of learning multiple languages since it offers that the grammar for all the languages is already inside one's head, hence one is just short to fill the gaps. All these theories are indispensable in this context as to explore how a human brain is stuck between priori and a priori perception of knowledge. Chomsky's transparent presentation of gripping ideas—from defining the [non] existence of language to the difference between national and literary language—is of paramount importance in this regard.

However, while directly addressing the question of melancholy adhered to the process of adaptation and assimilation of a language, I cannot exclude Jon Schumann's Acculturation Model which talks about the process by which immigrants pick up a new language. Bereft of following any syntactical or pedagogical ways of learning a language, Schumann focuses on the social and psychological aspects involved in language acquisition. He maintains how an individual finds it convenient to grasp a language if her own language and the target language are socially equal and have similar cultural layouts. The central argument is that language learning is not like mastering abstract subjects that can be learned from a book notwithstanding the world around you: the more one becomes familiar and adaptive to the immediate culture/social order the faster one grasps the new language. I will be enunciating how an individual goes through constant acculturation in order to situate oneself in a particular identity for national recognition.

Nationalism: Forsaking the Subaltern?

To have one language means there is at least one other language against which self- assertion is formulated. Imposition of any language over the other imbibes from the theory of social construction of nations as defined political entities that have limited geographical and demographic boundaries rather than organic, perpetual bodies.

In his *Imagined Communities*, Benedict Anderson theorizes a cultural conception of nationality and nationalism, asserting that the two '…are cultural artefacts of a particular kind' (Anderson 1983: 4). In an attempt to analyze the concept of nationalism, he puts forward the formation of a shared national identity. He describes the nation as an 'imagined political community—and imagined as both inherently limited and sovereign' (Anderson 1983: 6). He perceived the advent of the nation as a product of the print capitalism and media where the machinery of the printing press and the technology permitted overarching identity discourses to be published and circulated across diverse speech and languages granting similarity and dissemination of ideas affiliated to the nation. Suggesting that nations are much more than mere by-products of various identities, Anderson adduces that elites in decolonized countries had borrowed some forms of nationalism to appropriate others and to fashion their own.

Partha Chatterjee discusses this theory in his essay, "Whose Imagined Community?" (1996), where he contests Anderson and asserts that production of consent concerning the nation would imply a complete suppression of subaltern narratives, and simultaneous appropriation and accommodation of the same by the elites.

The fate of the untrained Indian speaker stuck between English elitism and Hindi chauvinism has given birth to this flummoxed body politic which invites the concerned scholar to raise some critical perspectives with theoretical reflections on various contemporary issues. To find out the core problem of the linguistic segregation, it demands tracing back to the roots of the history of language from the time when independent India was still struggling with the establishment of a common tongue which could help the nation define its identity.

The British English is invariably delegitimized in the nationalist context for being too visibly the language of the privileged and manifesting the pursuit of colonialism, whereas Indian English has consistently fallen prey to the hands of the whiner who strives to prove the utter redundancy of a language gaining supremacy which is learnt from the textbook and not spoken in the streets. On the other hand, the long-standing feud between Hindi and Urdu invites the scholar to frame new ideas to percolate into the psychological and intellectual domain of the common man who struggles to find a place without ascribing to the imperialism of the North India, or succumbing to a peripheral identity. Apart from the resistance from regional groups to Hindi's claim to power, there are representatives of multiple demography to whom the personal and the intellectual do not meet in seamless harmony.

As early as in March 1918, Mahatma Gandhi while chairing the 8th Hindi Sahitya Sammelan in Indore, publicly declared for the first time, that Hindi should be given the status of the country's national language. Gandhi sent five Hindi ambassadors, including his youngest son Devdas Gandhi, to Indian states where Hindi was not in vogue. Donning a traditional Kathiawadi pagdi, kurta and dhoti, the nation's beloved Bapu chaired this 'historic campaign. 'Like the way Britishers speak in English and use the same, I pray to all of you to provide Hindi the dignity of a national language...' DNA and thereby pleading the citizens to fulfill their duty. Gandhi, invoking the Ganga-Jamuna culture of Hindi, connoting the usage of Hindi by both the Hindu and the Muslim tongue, written in Nagari and Persian script, strongly advocated the use of Hindi in the functioning of courts.

Questioning the suitability of English as a national language, Gandhi mentioned the need of any national language to be treated as a compulsory subject. He expressed his fear by quoting the then Viceroy and his hope that English would gradually command a larger sphere, permeate family circle and finally rise to the status of a national language. Today's milieu supports this century-old viceregal contention, this prophecy of educated classes' dependency on English and all activities coming to a stand-still with the stop of English usage. Putting it to a credibility test of being the national language, Gandhi discarded the validity of English and legitimized Hindi with the belief that a national language should (a) be easy to learn, (b) have possibility of religious, commercial and political activity, (c) be the speech of the majority (Gandhi 1953) thereby championing the language understood and spoken by the majority.

Presenting the structural difficulties and grammatical disparity between Hindi and Dravidian languages, Gandhi catered the hardships to be confined to the learned class alone. He then approached and demanded help from the Dravidians to learn Hindi for the sake of proving their patriotism: 'We have a right to appeal to their patriotic spirit and expect them to put forth sufficient effort in order to learn Hindi. For in future, when Hindi has received state recognition it will be introduced as a compulsory language in

Madras as in other provinces' (Gandhi 1933). During Gandhi's visit to Cuttack, he was invited to solve a practical question regarding a tribe wedged between Hindi speaking people in Bihar and Oriya speaking people of then Orissa. He suggested 'the children should be taught Hindi, and naturally the script should be Devanagari.' He added, 'a spirit that is so exclusive and narrow as to want every form of speech to be perpetuated and developed is anti-national and anti-universal. All undeveloped and unwritten dialects should, in my humble opinion, be sacrificed and merged in the great Hindustani stream. It would be a sacrifice only to be nobler, not a suicide.' In order to make the cultured India flourish, he prescribed that people 'must arrest the growth of any process of disintegration or multiplication of languages and scripts' (Gandhi 1925: 74) along with upholding the image of Hindu India.

The fate of English as an 'imperial language, the language of diplomacy' was already prophesied by Gandhi, who also advocated the necessity of its knowledge, but to be preserved for certain upper caste and privileged classes. 'We are not jealous of English. All that is contended for is that it ought not to be allowed to go beyond its proper sphere. And as it will be the imperial language, we shall compel our Malaviyas, our Shastrias, and our Bannerjees to learn it. And we shall feel assured that they will advertise the greatness of India in other parts of the world.' This controversial statement is vehement enough to produce strong resentment in individuals sensitive to caste disparity.

Gandhi also supported North Indian chauvinism by suggesting the language that satisfies all conditions is 'Hindi which Hindus and Mohammedans in the North India speak and write' (*Young India*, August 27, 1925: 74). The kernel of growing melancholy from language submission could be mentioned in the same breath as Gandhi's discarding of Bengali or any other regional language. To reinforce his argument, Gandhi cherishes how normal it is to witness a Bengali speaking distorted Hindi when out of Bengal, while a Hindi- bhashi retaining his Hindi tongue across the borders is admirable. 'Even the unlettered Gujarati going to the North attempts to use a few Hindi words, whereas a gate-keeper from the North declines to speak in Gujarati even to his employer, who, on that account, has to speak to him in broken Hindi.' Gandhi goes to the extent of asking people to try employing Hindi even in the 'Dravid country'.

Talking of one nation, one language, yet segregating the southern part of India as a 'country' is revolting. The idea of this othering of the own inseparable part of India can also be studied in the light of racial segregation. Also the notion of Hindi usage in South India is conceived from the Madras passengers traveling by train, as he referred to in Young India. Travelers with the privilege and freedom of movement cannot represent the majority of South Indians. This sentiment can, perhaps, give rise to the strengthening of such humiliating stereotypes as South India comprises of only Madrasis, thereby discarding the existence and the contribution of Karnataka, Kerala, Andhra Pradesh (and the recently emerged Telangana).

The history of linguistic brawl in India can be dated back to the anti-Hindi agitation of 1937- 40, when series of protests took place in Madras Presidency of the British Raj. The battle was against introduction of compulsory Hindi in schools by Indian National Congress Party led by C. Rajagopalachari. Rajaji said in support of Hindi: 'only if we learn Hindi, the South Indian can gain respect among the others' (*Sudesamithran*, May 6, 1937). Alliance and followers of this ideological imposition were the pro-Hindi organizations, namely Hindustani Seva Dal, Hindustani Hitashi Sabha. A.T. Panneerselvam, the leader of the Justice Party, along with the Tamil Brigade, opposed this move and called for an anti-Hindi conference on October 4, 1937. But Rajaji went ahead and passed governmental order on compulsory Hindi on April 21, 1938. The move was immediately contested by E.V. Ramaswamy, widely known as Periyar, and the party Dravidar Kazhagam. The struggle witnessed three years of prolonged fasts, conferences, marches, picketing etc, resulting in a crackdown with two deaths and around twelve hundred people getting arrested including women and children. The mandatory Hindi was later withdrawn by the then British Governor of Madras, Lord Erskine, after resignation of Congress government in 1939.

This event had its stem from the 1918 mission undertaken by Mahatma Gandhi, viz. Dakshin Bharat Hindi Prachar Sabha, an organizational body established by Gandhi with the sole aim of propagating Hindi in South India. Gandhi as well as Jawaharlal Nehru were advocates of Hindi (or Hindustani, as Pandit Nehru believed) in non-Hindi speaking provinces. The idea was strongly rejected by Periyar who viewed it as an attempt to make Tamils (or Dravidians, for that matter) subordinate to the North Indians.

The most contemporary uprising to be invoked in this context is the recent series of cases involving anti-Hindi agitations in Karnataka. It took place in multiple phases, first when the banking forms in Kannada were replaced with Hindi forms, staffs not able to speak or understand Kannada posted in the banks of Karnataka, hence forcing the Kannadigas to learn Hindi or not to avail services, and also promoting Hindi by employing 'learn a Hindi word each day' tactics. Concerned activists took the campaign against this imposition to the streets and it flooded the social media on 11 July, 2017 with Twitter campaign under the hashtags, #NammaBankuKannadaBeku, #BankInMyLanguage under the aegis of Kannada Grahakara Koota. Earlier this year Indian Railways had stopped issuing ticket in Kannada which put the local passengers in many difficulties. This was later followed by renaming of signboards in Bengaluru Metro Rail, leading immediately to anti-Hindi agitation in June 2017 under the campaign #NammaMetroHindiBeda.

Karnataka Rakshana Vedike (KRV) members were seen defacing signboards in the silicone city of India. KRV had earlier emerged spreading terror through violent protests while the Cauvery water sharing dispute was on, and now causing havoc against Hindi imposition, by plastering signboards, tampering with hoardings of restaurants and banners in several metro stations including Chickpete. What amount of justification can be presented when KRV set Tamil Nadu trucks ablaze after the Supreme Court directed Karnataka Government to release Cauvery water to Tamil Nadu?

Role of the Right Wing in Hindi Imposition

Through their mouthpiece *Organiser* and *Panchajanya*, the RSS has been promoting Hindi hegemony in linguistic as well as in cultural spaces. *Organiser* first hit the stands back in 1947, just a few weeks before partition. In its sister-magazine, *Panchajanya's* Hindi divas edition, the editorial column blamed the Congress for lack of dedication to Hindi and for 'hatching conspiracy' to uphold other Indian languages against it, mentioning the Constitution maker's wish to replace English with Hindi or, as they claim, the national language. In defense, it states Hindi's unblemished impact on regional languages, whereas accusing the English speakers of still holding the desire for the country to remain enslaved. Invoking the wishes of Gandhi, Bose and Bhagat Singh, it poses English as an imposition, not a preference, asserting that India is yet to gain total independence. The debate of India vs Bharat is now English vs Hindi. While Hindi has public support, *janaadhaar*, English has market prominence and court privilege, namely *bazaar* and *durbar*.

The cover story of the June 2017 issue of *Panchajanya* claims that the reach of Indian language users is shooting up rapidly on the internet, predicting how in the coming five years every nine out of ten users of the internet will be taking recourse to their native tongue shrugging off English. Inciting the popularity of online shopping among the tech-savvy Indians, the writer celebrates the idea of taking selfies, uploading them on social media and encompassing the refashioning of the elderly lot using their native tongue in application based technology, in course manifesting how this is a new beginning for Indian languages (*Panchajanya*, June 11, 2017).

In the very next article, it talks about the dichotomy between English and Hindi, and promotes Hindi, thereby discarding the English speakers. In the same breath it claims that Hindi is a national language and anti-Hindi agitations are nothing but anti-national activities. It holds Nehru accountable for the deplorable status of Hindi for compromising with anti-Hindi elements which resulted in the growth of more anti-Hindi sentiments in the southern parts of India (Dwivedi 2017: 28). It claims that every language is given equal space in India but only Hindi has the strength to keep the nation united, and only Hindi can prevent the anglicization of Indian society. The magazine crudely mocks the southern Indian states who favored English instead of Hindi as their second language, thereby holding the latter responsible for bringing national shame. Invoking the post-independence decision of keeping English as an official language for ten years, Dwivedi claims how modern parents teach their kids 'mother, father' instead of 'maa, papa' (Ibid: p. 29). The very next article of this issue attacks the convent schools operated by Christian missionaries and accuses them of enforcing compulsory spoken English with monetary punishment. The article claims that different churches funded by foreign religious institutes are tampering with the Indian culture (*Panchajanya*, June 11, 2017).

It is interesting to note how a single edition of this magazine carry three back to back articles with a strategic move of imposing Hindi as the national language, firstly alluring the readers to their own native tongue, then to the devaluation of English and ultimately going straight away to blame a particular religious community for the disapproval of Hindi in the contemporary era.

The Hindiwallahs, as Alok Rai would prefer to call (2001: 5) celebrate September 14 as the Hindi Divas in order to 'save' Hindi. They begin with denying the need for a cultural argument for Hindi to be the national language, since they believe that it has already been made at lengths. Claiming that it is also not against the use of English but to emphasize the economic benefits of having Hindi as the national language, the writer defends why he writes in English instead of Hindi, claiming that 'the message needs to reach those who are fashionably Westernised and feel an extra pride in reading English only, who would even read Premchand in English' (*Bharat Niti,* Sep 13, 2016). The writer adds that this nation has for long debated 'the need to have a national language and English has always been thrusted upon crores of masses by the imperial masters and later on by the succeeding governments, the historic debates in Parliament over why Hindi should not be our national language, the thrust of Nehru towards retaining English as the language of transaction across the nation' (Ibid).

Chomsky, in this regard, advances some interesting theories. For him, the idea of a national language is a pretty modern phenomenon. He connects this concept with the rise of nationalism, communication etc. He mentions: 'You have to learn the national language when you go to school, while it is a different language, the one you speak at home' (Chomsky 1989). When we talk about language change, it cannot be merely seen in the light of learning a new medium of expression. What actually happen is that some kind of species is changing. There is an amalgamation of all sorts of dialects over time, either because of conquest, some political changes or boundaries drawn in different places, or some kind of commercial interchange. Between generations there are usually miniscule changes having to do with other influences from the outside, leading to dramatic alterations.

In the question of homogeneity of a language, Chomsky mentions how English is relatively homogenous, sharing in this regard, how he could go a long way in the United States and yet how fluently he could understand everybody's speech. This is not true for the rest of the world. There are enough national unities at the present time, so one can find a border with ease, but going back somewhat further when there was no geographical border, constant change and fluctuations took place, if not continuum. Languages speaking at different places are often not mutually intelligible. With the rise of national states, advancement of national communication and insertion of the national education system appeared the concept of national language. Chomsky describes the unusualness of English by enunciating how in the pre-colonial times, there were hundreds and thousands of different languages in what is now called the United States of America. Through the destruction of indigenous population, which was kind of genocidal at times, the conquest by speakers of basically one group ended up having a large homogenous language, namely English.

The Myth of Pure Language

Virtually every national language, every national culture (especially the European ones), has a mythology that theirs' is the only real, pure language and all the others are corrupt. If I could invoke here the age old debate of French purity and English redundancy, I would add that Chomsky quoted a famous French linguist on how he prophesied that French will be the language of science, while German and English will be the language of literature. The reason put forth is, French is clear with the words following the order of thoughts, while German and English do not follow any such order. So it is generally assumed by the advocates of French purity that French is good for telling the truth, while German and English are good languages for telling fantasies or concocting falsehoods. The mythology of purity, lucidity, clarity of any culture goes back to the idea of certain dominance for these attitudes to get established. Raising the debate of English as a pure language, Chomsky questions the concept of purity and whether Shakespearean English could be called pure. Discarding the homogenous definition of 'language', by saying 'there is no such thing as a language', he supports his statement by adding that there are just many different ways of speaking that people have.

In addressing the question of linguistic power and prestige, the most intriguing query is how a language gains supremacy. This may well be explained in such a fashion that the speech of a conquering community, or a wealthy group, or priestly caste of high order deciding that certain languages are good and assigning the others as bad ones. But what happens when the social and political relations are reversed? The answer is that we make opposite conclusions. For instance, Black English is never regarded as quite proper English. On the other hand, if Blacks happened to have all the power and Whites were working for them then Black English would have been celebrated worldwide and would enjoy the status as English does today.

The same discourse exists between Hindi, Urdu, Hindustani, which, if spoken as one and synonymous, is a hybrid language that had absorbed the semantic resources of many traditions. Alok Rai (2001) laments the loss of Hindi to the Hindi chauvinists or the Hindiwallahs, and invites the readers to explore how 'a popular language came to be fractured, splitting the language community into warring groups with opposing identities'... how 'systems of segregation in schools, and the nature of textbooks produced by Pandits and Maulvis, deepened the linguistic divide' (Bhattacharya 2001: viii). Although having emerged from a common origin, Hindi and Urdu/Hindavi have often suffered socio-political blows following a clearly discernible fate, by the twentieth century, as two independent languages, as modern Hindi and modern Urdu.

Grierson's Hindi 'is a Persian, not an Indian word, and properly signifies a native of India, as distinguished from a 'Hindu' or non-Musalman Indian. ...In this sense, Bengali and Marathi are as much Hindi as the language of the Doab' (Grierson 1968). Rahul Sankrityana's Hindi is the *ur*-language whose modern form may be considered under two aspects: 'A widely disseminated Khari Boli and the various local languages which are spoken in different places: Magahi, Bhojpuri, Banarasi, Avadhi, Kannauji, Brajmandali, etc...' (Sankrityayan 1937: 231). Gyan Chand, an eminent Urdu scholar claims: 'It is absolutely clear that Urdu and Hindi are not two separate languages. To call them two languages is to belie all principles of linguistics and to deceive oneself and others' (Chand 1974).

Urdu written in Persian script and Hindi written in Devanagari cannot attest the existence of two separate languages. Similarly, Urdu composed of more Arabic and Persian words while Hindi laden with more of Sanskrit cannot alter the complex linguistic intermingling of Hindi/Hindavi, the rudimentary vocabulary of both the languages being the same. Malaysia and Indonesia have one language called Malay, written in the Arabic and Roman script respectively. This does not imply that they are two distinct languages. Pre-partition Punjabi Muslims wrote Punjabi in Urdu script, the Sikhs in Gurumukhi, and the Hindus in Devanagari, this did not mean they wrote three languages (Ibid). Ram Bilas Sharma observes—'Hindi and Urdu are not two separate languages;

they are basically one and the same. Their pronouns, verbs, and basic vocabulary are the same. There are no two other languages in the world whose pronouns and verbs are one hundred percent the same. Russian and Ukranian are much akin to each other but even they are not so closely alike' (Sharma 1978: 288).

In order to study the disparity present in the debate of language, education and nationalism in India, an attempt to explore ideological underpinnings and the agency of the Indian government in framing the language policies at the school level is required. From appointing members of council or editorial boards of premier institutes that provide higher education to revising textbooks in schools run by state governments, there is an all—pervading encroachment of the majoritarian mainstream Hindi culture in educational structure. Amartya Sen in an interview with the NDTV claims that there is a clear pattern of Hindutva in the appointments of key educational and cultural institutions (Sen 2015). In addressing the issue of melancholy in the context of linguistic dissension, this chapter specifically aims at how melancholy works in the construction of nonconformist and aberrant cultural rendition, both as collective endeavor and individual struggle in public and private space. Apart from making an effort to study the lived yet relatively undocumented trains of memories and experiences, this chapter tries to attempt an intervention of social media representations to situate the multiple episodes of crisis and sustained political submission in the domain of socio-linguistic battle.

'How to Love Without Getting Hurt?'[2]

Conventionally the concept of language could be posited in three contexts: mother tongue/colloquial, national/political, and academic/literary. In school, one learns the literary language which one does not encounter in the streets. Nobody teaches you your mother tongue; it automatically grows in your head. The question of national language has been increasingly recognized as a locus of dispute, therefore becoming a room of intrusion less by linguists and more by politicians and civil society activists. The tussle starts when the system that grows in your head is different from the system which is regarded as necessary, appropriate, proved, and a prestigious dialect. Who determines that prestige? The very fact that we have to 'teach' people is because it is artificial; it is not the language they are born with. Hence, rather than linguistic apprehension, the driving mechanism is mostly socio-political.

Disenchantment (with Hindi) and marginality (from English) imparts melancholia and makes the subject (feel) an outsider. Talking of individual/personal acculturation, one can take an account of her own estrangements—for a person, say, hailing from a small town of India, Bhojpuri accent in a Hindi school, Hindi accent in an English college/university—the passage from local to state, state to national, (and to international) yields an individual skeptical of the modernization ritual of educational institutions.

In this regard, I would like to bring the not long past tragic events of suicides by two research scholars, one which stirred the nation with outrage and the other which was swept under the carpet. I do not intend to inculpate any party for these two deaths, but my inquisitiveness springs from the language they used in the social media to communicate with the outer world. Rohith Vemula, a 26 year old research scholar enrolled in the Central University of Hyderabad (HCU), hanged himself in the winter of 2016 leaving behind a suicide letter. In the following year, Muthukrishnan, another research scholar in Jawaharlal Nehru University (JNU), New Delhi hanged himself in a similar manner on Holi.

It was only after Vemula had a brawl with the right wing affiliated students, that he along with four other PhD students (Dontha Prashant, Sunkannya Velpula, Vijay Kumar and Sheshu Chemdugunta) was suspended from the university and barred from the hostel. This struggle was basically against such an organization which mainly upholds the North Indian majoritarian mainstream Hindu-Hindi culture and the response from that organization and the ruling establishment in the Capital was merely a symbol of the biased approaches against non-Hindi minority culture. It was shocking to note that the kind of response he received from the state was undemocratic in nature and clearly politically motivated.

In his letter to the Vice-Chancellor, Vemula condemns injustice meted out to the lower caste students inside the university campuses and demanded that Dalit students should be given 'a nice rope' (Vemula, hang themselves. It did not end there. He was portrayed antinational and was denied his Dalit identity posthumously and his mother had to go through streams of humiliation when the State tried to prove that he did not belong to the Dalit community. This establishes how anybody who does not accept the mainstream majoritarian Brahminical idea of nation is branded as anti- national.

What was most remarkable about Vemula's letter was his choice of writing the endnote in a tongue acquired and not born with. His melancholy seemed to rub the words he wrote, making them almost tangible. His irrepressible despondency makes his words penetrate our thoughts, unlatching the reflective ideologies or spaces that would be forever dedicated to his renunciation. Calling his birth 'a fatal accident' (Ibid), it can be assumed that this letter was intended to globally serve the purpose of bridging the gap between the English speaking class and the deprived class people like himself, who strive all their life to gain command over a non-native tongue.

A flipping through his account in the social media would raise certain compelling points. The use of photographs of Hollywood actors, South Indian heroes, Manga characters and Aaron Swartz as display pictures clearly denotes that he did not embrace any north Indian notion of nationalism. His whole life can be regarded as an emblem of resistance to the mainstreaming of his identity. Not many years back, he had posted pictures of his home with a sewing machine as the sole bread winner before he had started availing Junior Research Fellowship which went viral. One can find pictures of a small dingy kitchen and tiny corners of his home published in social media a few years before his death. His excitement knew no bounds after getting through HCU that he posted photographs of each nook of his hostel room, perhaps proving his belief in the power of 'stardust'[3]. We may now find ourselves in a state to comprehend why exactly Vemula, in his farewell letter, says: 'May be I was wrong, all the while, in understanding the world. ...In understanding love, pain, life, death' (Ibid).

The concept of the nation emerging in the saffron regime as a socio-political structure to replace the previous orders with the insertion of constitutional alterations has given a new order of conceptualizing the center's sovereignty or the North Indian rule representing a handful of population limited to a defined demography and territory over which the state, in the disguise of nationalism, can exercise absolute power.

Muthukrishnan or Rajni Krish's Facebook post was addressed to such hegemonic nationalist structures. He writes: 'Dear anti-nationals, let me tell you, one day this nation's leader is going to sell all. Just for a selfie and for a standing ovation from the outsiders. Hundreds and hundreds of Appa Raos are going to kill thousands of Rohiths and they are going to say, 'He/she was a gifted student'. All the intellectuals from the marginalized communities will get arrested just for mocking fictional characters. At the same time, all the leading national institutes will be headed by people who cannot even clear the 10th standard exam. These people claim dissenters as anti-nationals and seditious. They are going to kill many Rohiths like us, just for eating beef, for being rational, for being intellectually productive for the country. But we are the real sons of this land and after we are killed, there will be no nation' (Rajini Krish, Facebook Post, Jan 2016).

People's reaction after Krish's death dealt basically with the struggles he faced all his life for being a Tamil speaker and contesting the English tongue. He himself had expressed many a times how his incompetence in English hindered his way of accomplishments. In his display picture in social media, he wrote the story of his own struggle of getting through JNU. Standing in front of the Nehru statue inside the University campus, he remembers how he appeared four times for the JNU Entrance exam but owing to his poor English skills he could not get through but still he would not give up. He admits having saved pennies just to visit JNU and recalls how in '[one of the] interview[s], after 11 minutes, one madam told me that I am speaking simple language. This year interview I spoke, I answered all the questions, three professors told me that you spoke well. Now I realize that I am the only one from Government Arts College [who] came to study in central university and I am the only one from Selam district who got selected in JNU. I wrote a proposal for the Centre for Historical Studies (JNU) eight times and finally I got through' (Rajini Krish, Facebook Post, July 26, 2016). He also talks about how he desired to record the historical moment of his accomplishment in a book which he wished to name 'A Junket to JNU'.

The two events of suppressed melancholy and sustained internal violence referred to above were disturbing both for the individual and the collective. In such perception, one crucial context would be the moments of self-expression, sometimes through social media, and sometimes through tying a rope around the neck, in which the personal and the conventional patterns of continuity were breached by the hegemonic intervention, in which the general public became both a witness to as well as a reluctant participant in an unprecedented specter of melancholia. Another key context would be the post- violence period. The idea is to understand what these people did to confront the trauma they experienced as individuals or communities. In the general psychological or anthropological understanding of the term, a trauma is an extremely painful event in the life of an individual or collective, that due to its very intensity, does not allow an individual's or society's routine skills or capabilities to deal with (Perera 2016: 8). The concept of trauma in academic discourse seems to have undergone a shift in emphasis and in the recent years, it is realized as a need for representation and the refusal to be represented (Roth and Salas 2001: 2). It was only recently that the study of trauma and melancholy moved away from the ramparts of psychological and medical sciences and entered the discourses of humanities.

So what exactly are we to do with the suffering of the dispossessed and what constitutes their melancholy? For most individuals any exploration into the subjects' memory and melancholy through their private and public manifestations cannot be an undemanding academic enquiry. We cannot afford to stay detached from the reality of this melancholy and take refuge within the bastion of psychological objectivity beyond a line. Dealing with contemporary issues of linguistic conflicts is a matter of living in the domains of memory, melancholy and erasure, encompassed by narrative discourses of dejection rooted to a common past of suffering. These gestures of melancholy may come to us in the form of visible social media accounts, and many people in the private domain will continue to remember them. It is important for the collective to realize that the suffering is not over.

From the beginning of Indian history, several individuals, communities have questioned and challenged authority—be it the state, political or religious hegemonies, caste dominion, gender hierarchies or even the idea of theology. Dissension has persisted despite all attempts made to exterminate it. The Constitution of India, in 1950, assembled a country to be a democratic republic, thereby guaranteeing every citizen the right to express and assuring them the freedom of life and faith, with an oath to uphold the Indian tradition of plurality and dissension. Yet, it has not been an easy task to safeguard these freedoms since the conduct of the state, often working in the interest of political parties, has been deceitful and dishonest. In the contemporary times, these conundrums have taken violent and barbaric dimensions. The self-styled custodians of mainstream majoritarian culture have mowed down the dispossessed for asking what is rightfully theirs. While memory and melancholy may be private at one level, it is often perpetuated and appropriated by the state machineries. Many decades after the independence, the zeal of democracy is sabotaged again by the Hindu majoritarian political forces. The recent branding of universities as anti-national hubs, the witch-hunting of political speakers and scholars, the atrocities against the caste, communal and linguistic minorities, the rampant killings of activists and innocents, sometimes in the name of 'love-jihad' while at others under the crime of beef-eating, have testified that the present regime has all the right to crush the dreams of democracy and dissent. This has much to do with the incessant effort of spreading a large-scale amnesia regarding our social and cultural history. While the murders of rationalists, intellectuals and creative dissenters (Narendra Dabholkar, Govind Pansare, M.M. Kalburgi, Gauri Lankesh) are revolting, what is more inexcusable is the silence of the larger section of the population which is causing continual support to the tormentors' regime. There is a pressing need for public condemnation of these atrocious acts to prevent dissent from dying. For the Indian languages to survive, we need more Ganesh Devys[4] who dedicate their lives to preserve the vanishing cultures of India. To wipe out the melancholy from thousands of Rohiths and Krishs, we have to work against the interests of socio-political regimes who threaten not only dissent or opposition, but also independent thought. This is only to ensure Rohith's stardust and to ensure Krish's junket.

Notes

1. Coined by Chomsky, the phrase refers to the Socratic dialogue, *Meno*, implying the problem of explaining how we can know so much given so little evidence.
2. This phrase is taken from Rohith Vemula's suicide letter.
3. Taken from Rohith Vemula's suicide letter.
4. Ganesh Narayan Das, former professor of English, a renowned literary critic and activist and founder director of the Bhasha Research and Publication Center, Vadodara and *Adivasi Academy* at Tejgadh, Gujarat, who established to create a unique educational environment for the study of tribal communities.

References

Anderson, Benedict, *Imagined Communities: Reflections on the Origin and Spread of Nationalism* (London: Verso, 1983).

Anderson, Benedict, *Language and Power: Exploring Political Cultures in Indonesia* (New York: Cornell University Press, 1990).

Apparasu, Srinivasa Rao, "JNU Suicide: Dalit Scholar was Rohith Vemula's friend at Hyderabad University", March 27, 2017.

"Bengaluru Hindi Language Row: Karnataka Rakshana Vedike Members Deface Signboard in Tech City." *Financial Express*, July 6, 2017.

Chand, Gyan, "Urdu Hindi ya Hindustani", *Hindustani Zaban*, Jan-April 1974.

Chomsky, Noam, Interview with Al Page, in *Upon Reflection*, University of Washington, UWTV Classics, 1989.

Descartes, René, and Donald A. Cress, *Discourse on Method; and: Meditations on First Philosophy* (Indianapolis: Hackett Pub, 1998).

Dwivedi, Piyush, "Angrezi maansikta nahin, Hindi chahiye", *Panchajanya,* June 11, 2017, p. 28.

FP Staff, "Gauri Lankesh Murder was Worryingly Similar to Govind Pansare, Narendra Dabholkar and M.M. Kalburgi killings," *Firstpost,* Sep 07, 2017.

Gandhi, M.K., *Towards New Education*, ed. Bharatan Kumarappa (Ahmedabad: Navajivan Mudranalaya, Jitendra T. Desai, 1953).

Gandhi, M.K., "Hindi: The National Language for India" in *Speeches and Writings of Mahatma Gandhi,* 4th ed. 395-99 (Madras: G.A. Natesan and Co.: 1933).

Gandhi, M.K., *Young India,* August 27, 1925, p. 74.

Grierson, George, *Linguistic Survey of India,* Vol. 9, Part 1, 1st edn, 1916; rpt, Delhi, 1968.

"Hindi Signboards on Bengaluru Metro lead to Protest." *News 18*, June 21, 2017.

Kannabiran, Kalpana, "Post Truths about Rohith Vemula." *The Hindu*, Jan 17, 2017.

"Karnataka: No to Metro Boards in Hindi, say Kannada activists." *Deccan Chronicle*, June 23, 2017.

"Karnataka's Anti-Hindi Row now Includes English as Well." *The New Indian Express*, July 06, 2017.

"Language War: Pro-Kannada activists to Team Up with DMK to Protest Imposition of Hindi." *Hindustan Times*, July 03, 2017.

Locke, John, *Essay Concerning Human Understanding* (Hernnstein and Murray, 1994).

Mondal, Sudipto. "Rohith Vemula: An Unfinished Portrait." *Hindustan Times,* http://www.hindustantimes.com/static/rohith-vemula-an-unfinished-portrait/.

Rai, Alok, *Tracts for the Times: Hindi Nationalism*, ed. Neeladri Bhattacharya (New Delhi: Orient Blackswan, 2001).

Raghuvanshi, Sanket, "The Economics of Hindi as national Language", *Bharat Niti,* Sep 13, 2016.https://www.bharatniti.in/article/the-economics-of-hindi-as-national-language/460.

Sankrityayan, Rahul, *Puratatva Nibandhavali* (Allahabad: Indian Press, 1937) p. 231.

Sen, Amartya, 'RSS Attack on IIM, IIT: Prime Minister Modi, the Sangh Parivar will Destroy Your 'Make in India Dream", Reported in *Firstpost* (online media portal), July 21, 2015.

Sharma, Ram Bilas, *Bharat ki Bhasha Samasya,* New Delhi, 1978.

Skinner, B.F., *The Behavior of Organisms: An Experimental Analysis* (New York: Appleton Century Crofts, 1938).

Sudhir, Uma, "My Name is Rohith Vemua. I Am a Dalit", he said in Video days before he died," ed. Shuchi Shukla, *NDTV,* 17 Oct 2016.

Vemula, Rohith, "Letter to the Vice Chancellor: Solution for Dalit Problem", Dec 18, 2015.

Verma, Reshu, "Bolne laga Bharat", *Panchajanya*, June 11, 2017.

"When Mahatma Gandhi's Heart called for Making Hindi a National Language." *DNA India,* Indore, Press Trust of India, 14 Sep 2014.

*The Melancholic Name**

Saitya Brata Das

> So I renounced and sadly see:
> Where the word breaks off no thing may be.
>
> —Stefan George, *The Word*

Poesis

In the last pages of *Philosophical Inquiries into the Nature of Human Freedom*, Schelling writes,

> In God, too, there would be a depth of darkness if he did not make the condition his own and unite it to him as one and as absolute personality. Man never gains control over the condition even though in evil he strives to do so; it is only *loaned* to him independent of him; hence his personality and selfhood can never be raised to complete actuality. This is the sadness which adheres too all finite life, and inasmuch as there is even in God himself a condition at least relatively independent, there is in him, too, a source of sadness which, however, never attains actuality but rather serves for the eternal joy of triumph. Thence the veil of sadness, which is spread over all nature, the deep unappeasable melancholy of all life. (Schelling 1936: 79)

* This article is previously published in *Journal for Cultural Studies*, 11:2 (2007), 111-123.

In all our finite life, in our sense of finitude, in our never being able to attain actuality to make our condition our own, to *own* our condition, to make it our "proper" of the very "proper", to make it our "present" to ourselves: this is the sadness of our finite life, insofar as our condition is "loaned" to us, so Schelling says, "gifted" to us independently of us. The condition of our being, never being able to be actualized completely, remains non-appropriable to us, as if the ground of our being escapes all grounding, and yet gives us all grounding, that must be other than ground. Schelling calls this unground (*abgrund*): the unconditioned not opposite to conditions, but that precisely gives the possibility of all conditions, and yet is heterogeneous to all conditions, that exceeds all conditions. How to think this impossible thought, this madness of thought? To put it another way, in another register, another language: how to think the undecidable that is heterogeneous to all decisions, and yet never opposite to decisions, but rather the other way, decisions are possible precisely at the very moment, *at the limit* and out of the undecidable; that decisions are to be possible, one must pass through the undecidable, must traverse the experience of the impossible. Otherwise there are no decisions but programmatic, already calculated, projected, teleological installations of already determined results: in other words, it will be without, to use a phrase of Derrida, the "surprise of the event", it will be closed to the "event" itself which is nothing but surprise, the surprise of the coming of the event, and the event of surprise. Coming surprises us, because it cannot be programmed, projected in advance, in other words, it is incalculable, which does not preclude calculations, but precisely demands them, that there must be calculations, the calculating the incalculable—for there is no question of calculating the calculable. The event, the incalculable coming of the Other, surprises us precisely because there are calculations and precisely because event is otherwise than calculations, because the event is heterogeneous to all calculations that there is surprise. Yet decisions do not exhaust the event, or the event is not exhausted in decisions, though decisions are always made in the name of the event, in the event of justice and because of this inexhaustibility of the event, and the inexhaustibility of justice in the works of actualization, which means in the works of law and in the works of decisions, event overflows all works of actualization, justice overflows all works of law, the incalculability of surprise overflows all calculability of decisions. Therefore there is future, there is the *yet to come*, there comes the event and there is justice: it is this Derrida calls, 'messianic without messianism', so that the inexhaustibility of justice *yet to come* calls for decisions, calculations and negotiations—*in the name of justice*. Justice is non-appropriable because it comes from elsewhere, otherwise than "present", because justice is "loaned" to "me" by the other, because decisions are finite, conditioned, limited. In other words justice is nothing but a "loan", I am underscoring Schelling's word here, or justice as gift. The gift is the gift of justice—later we will speak of the gift of the name—the time of this gift is not exhausted by any presence of self-presence, since it is coming from the other, otherwise than presence, the gift is always already untimely. *The gift does not happen in time*: the time of the gift is a time "out of joint": caesural, dehiscent movement of deferring. Yet it happens, it happens "here" and "now", but a "here" which is otherwise than any topology, or rather it is *a-topos* (my coinage), which is not opposed to topology, and a "now" which is otherwise than "present" of the self-present, a "now" which is not present in presence. Without this gift of the caesural, without this future of the coming, without the justice otherwise than "present", or "given", without this opening to the other, there is neither politics, nor ethics, but only calculations without promise, laws without justice, decisions without future and gifts without the other, otherwise than calculations. Decisions are *not* between two equally opposed choices, (even when God decided to reveal himself, Schelling says, to be actualized himself, he did not make choices, but choices emanate from him, from the very nature of his necessity) which can have a mediating term to unify or reconcile the two, so that *Aufhebung*, sublation, be accomplished: decisions are decisions between the undecidable and the decidable, to negotiate the non-negotiable and negotiable, that must traverse the undecidability of the two—between the undecidable and the decidable.

But why invoke Schelling here? Why mourning and the name? How to think of the gift of the name, of language? How to think of an unground, the *abgrund* that is not simply opposed to ground, but gives ground, gives the grounding of all grounds and yet is heterogeneous to all grounds? Or, to put it in a language more in tune with Schelling's, how to think of the possibilities of conditioned being, our conditioned finite existence—and since conditioned being, being conditioned, cannot appropriate its condition, whose condition is a "loan", a "debt"? How to think this conditioned existence whose condition is not exhausted in the conditioned, a condition that is otherwise than any conditionality, the *abgrund*? This is the most singular critique of Hegel, that opens the system up to what Schelling refers to as the "already always", and also to the "*yet to come*"—*the immemorial past of the gift* and *the futurity of the event*—since conditioned existence cannot appropriate its condition, cannot actualize it, it remains open to the infinite possibilities of creations and freedom. In other words, abgrund does not undermine, negate, or even minimize freedom; rather the other way, *abgrund* is what calls for freedom, or rather calls itself forth in acts of revealing, that calls forth acts of actualizations, to the infinite possibilities of freedom, to the labour of effective actions. If an "unappeased melancholy" adheres to all our finite life, being finite and conditioned being that we are who cannot appropriate our own condition once and for all, it is this very melancholy that calls forth, each moment and singularity, the joyous acts of creation as infinite, inexhaustible, never-once-and-for-all actualizable acts of freedom. Therefore Aristotle says of all creative people—philosophers, poets and statesmen—are essentially melancholic (Aristotle 1971: 953–57). Since poets work and create at the very abyss of opening, which is the opening of the world that is revealed in the destinal becoming of the world, in its eternal coming to be, that withdraws from and yet revealed in "world"—this work, as an experience of impossibility, of the abyss of the *abgrund* or *unground*, is an experience of mourning. A fundamental note of sadness and melancholy adheres to all works. It is in this sense that all works are works of mourning. Perhaps it is in this sense that Derrida says,

> … All work is also the work of mourning. All work in general works *at mourning*. In and of itself. Even when it has the power to give birth, even and especially when it plans to bring something to light and let it be seen. The work of mourning is not one kind of work among other possible kinds: an activity of the kind "work" is by no means a specific figure for production in general… that is why whoever thus works at the work of mourning learns the impossible—and that mourning is interminable. Inconsolable. Irreconciliable. (Derrida 1996: 172)

Since the philosophical discourse of totality, or the system that forms the "world" of signification, cannot posit this opening as eternal past—for it must already be granted, "loaned" to its possibility by the opening that has *already always* become the eternal past of the system that never ceases to be past—the opening of the world cannot be posited within the philosophical discourse of totality, or within the world. This is said by Schelling without saying. But he says, and he says of God: 'God is not a system but a life' (Schelling 1936: 78). Poets work and their work is the work of mourning. The *abgrund*, the unground which is simultaneously the ground and opening of the world, *loans* us our existence as gift, and our finite existence, therefore, carries the lament of the opening, of the scission, of the spacing, of the caesura within it as attunement, or as what Heidegger calls the "fundamental tone of sadness". That means that a tone of melancholy is already always the attunement in the very heart of opening of our existence. In the very opening of existence—for existence is the gift of the finitude, the *loan*, the debt that we inherit, the gift that is given whose condition cannot be appropriated—there lies the infinite tone of sadness. Therefore the works of poets that struggle to articulate the opening of the world and in this very articulation opens the world thereby, the world does not have a place for these poets. As unground of opening is already withdrawn from the world that is opened by this opening, poets are therefore a the strangers to the world, lonely, and homeless. Heidegger says in the *Introduction to Metaphysics*:

> The *polis* is the historical place, the there *in* which, *out* of which, and *for* which history happens. To this place and scene of history

> belong the gods, the temples, the priests, the festivals, the games, the poets, the thinkers, the rulers, the council of elders, the assembly of people, the army and the fleet. All this does not first belong to the *polis*, does not become political by entering into relation with a statesman and a general and the business of the state. No, it is political, i.e. at the site of history, provided there be (for example) poets *alone,* but then really poets, priests *alone,* but then really priests, rulers *alone* but then really rulers. Be, this means: as violent men to use power, to become pre-eminent in historical being as creators, as men of action. Pre-eminent in the historical place, they become at the same time *apolis,* without city and place, lonely, strange, alien and uncanny, without issue amid the beings as a whole, without stature and limit, without structure and order, because they themselves as creators must first create all this. (Heidegger 1999: 152)

This dense paragraph from Heidegger problematizes the complex relationship between the *poesis* of the opening, the hiatus, the cut that opens the *polis* and the political ontology of the world, the political being of the *polis*, which must already have been opened by the opening falling outside the *polis*: in the very opening of *polis,* poets have already always become strangers to *polis*, have become homeless and exiled, have been thrown outside the *polis.* Therefore the opening of the *polis* is simultaneously a concealing, or excluding of the very poets whose works—the works of opening—open to all works. This means the *polis* too has its eternal past which cannot be posited within itself, but *loaned* to it: the *polis* does not exist before being political, but rather *polis* is—the fleet, the assembly of the wise, the festivals and harvest—political insofar as the very opening of the *polis* is exiled or concealed as *apolis*, beyond its boundary of the historico-territorial that comes to be in this opening. The melancholy of this rupture, the scission that marks the opening—so that there may be the *polis*—the marks whose absent origin haunts the destinal becoming of world, the coming to be of existing, carries the trace of this rupture in every work of the historical world of signification, opening the *polis* to the outside, that is, to the opening itself, the *apolis*, which is not apolitical. This also means: opening, that is at once closed, is at the same time, also to remain opened to the opening. Opening opens the *polis* to its finite existing, but the *polis* carries the traces of its own finitude in mourning and in mourning, remains open to its opening—to its eternal past, not the past that *has been*, that was present, but infinite past, which it cannot posit within the *polis* as its self-present past. Language of the world, its labour to constitute sense, itself carries this lament of the opening, lament for what is already-always excluded from the world as eternal past which the world cannot posit within itself and cannot appropriate, as if, as it were, in this very work of signification, the absent origin itself (in being signified and named too much, in being too much presented and represented and for the very reason presented too little, announcing the finitude of the opening, for there is no signification without thereby announcing the finitude of the opening) laments in the overwhelming work of significations of finite beings—in signification itself.

Lichtung

Elsewhere Heidegger thinks of this opening as *Lichtung*: since there are beings, since there is a play of light and darkness, there must already be an opening for the light: 'whether or not what is present is experienced, comprehended or presented, presence as lingering in openness always remains dependent upon the prevalent opening. What is absent, too, cannot be as such unless it presences in the *free space of the opening*' (Heidegger 1978: 386). How to think this opening, the spacing—the poesis of spacing—for there to be polis: this thinking of the political—I would say deconstruction is nothing but thinking of the political—so that there be polis, coming to existence of polis, so that there be effectivity and effectuation of our historical existence, this thinking of the political demands that there be deconstruction of a certain dominant determination of politics. This thought of coming and opening for there to be *polis*, and politics (if that means effectuations of our historical world), is essentially an experience of mourning: all works—of effective actualization of the world—work at this mourning, that means, work at the finitude that opens the world, that finitude that spaces and calls forth polis, so that there be the future of the coming. There is future, the coming of the event, and the *yet to come* of justice because all works of actualization are conditioned, finite and cannot exhaustibly exhaust the justice to be actualized, which means, justice is always yet to be actualized, yet to be accomplished, while always been accomplished. If I use Schelling's words, 'all existence must be conditioned in order that it may be actual, that is personal, existence. God's existence, too, could not be personal if it were not conditioned, except that he has the conditioning factor within himself and not outside himself' (Schelling 1936: 79). *The there* of opening, in the opening for the coming, is already always, thereby lapsed in an infinite, immemorial past—Schelling refers to "eternal past"—outside time, *the* opening of the world that is always already excluded, concealed, forgotten, lost without recuperation and re-appropriation[1]. Therefore mourning is inconsolable and infinite. It is mourning for the others who are already always dead, in an un-localizable, non-self-present, in-a-never-present time, or, rather, who is lost outside time; others who are lost in the very opening of the world, in the opening of existence, those who have become homeless and exiled and have become strangers to us. (In Parenthesis: It is in this sense, if I am permitted to use the word, that the death of the other is not simply "empirical", which is to say that the time of the other's death is not "my" time, it is not the time of self-presenting presence, it is not a "localizable", "identifiable" loss: the other does not die in time, that doesn't mean that it occurs in some transcendental eternity, but that the death of the other is the "already-already" time of the end of time, each time, singular time, it is the end of the singular end of the singular world. Perhaps it is in this sense that Derrida uses the title of a book as *Each Time the End of the World.* Death already always works in life, while still living—in the lives of friends: mourning is inconsolable, not only because he dies, if I can still use the word, (but I am putting it within comma) "empirically", but also that even before death, death already always unworks his/her works. It is this already always of death, I am reminded of Blanchot's distinction between dying and death, that this death—unlocalizable, untimely, non-negative dying—it is this death of the other whose "mourning", says Derrida, 'constitutes friendship' (Derrida 1996: 188), the immemorial, irrecuperable already dying of the other, that the "now" dying of the Other is not-contemporaneous with the time of the present, that the relationship with the Other, even while the Other still being "empirically" (one must be aware that the concept "empirical" has its history, one that is metaphysical, and deconstructible) alive, is a relationship with a certain absence, his absence in "my" time of "presence". This also means friendship is not possible, in other words, experience of friendship is not an order of "possibility" but rather an experience of impossibility of all possibilities, as Blanchot says, it is a community, community of friends, which is unavowable. This mourning, for the Other's finitude, is inconsolable, for the Other is already always absent from any self-presence of the present, since "I" am only the latecomer, the survivor, the "inheritor"—in Specters of Marx, Derrida evokes this figure of "inheritor"—which means, the time of presence is already late in relationship to a certain "now" of the Other, in a disjunctive time. Responsibility is always responsibility of the inheritor, the latecomer, and the survivor.)

It is in this inconsolable mourning for the other's death—*not my death*—that there is a responsibility to the other, justice to the other who is already always dead, or who is yet come, in other words, to the other whose death is noncontemporaneous with any present. In the very beginning of *Spectres of Marx*, Derrida writes:

> No justice—let us not say no law and once again we are not speaking here of laws—seems possible or thinkable without the principle of some *responsibility*, beyond all living present, within that which disjoins the living present, before the ghosts of those who are not yet born or who are already dead… (Derrida 1994: xix)

What would the political be without the opening for the coming—the *poesis* of the opening that opens *being-towards-the-others* that constitutes or deconstitutes *polis*, the community that cannot be avowed and that inoperates while operating all the time, community that has already always unworked so that there be works, existence that is already always ungrounded so that there be grounds—and that this opening to the other is nothing but an impossible experience of finitude, always another's, beyond my death, a mourning beyond consolation? How to think this impossible thought, the impossibility of thinking? What the political would be without madness—a certain madness? A certain madness of thinking. A certain madness of finite thinking, or thinking of finitude. A certain madness of mourning.

Gift

If mourning marks or traces the very scission, the interruption of the inappropriable and the call for appropriability, it is the very condition, in its unconditionality, of the political: the political inscribes, installs, erects over a ground that ex-cribes itself, disinstalls itself, desists and ex-appropriates itself. Without this excess, without this ex-appropriation, without the non-appropriability of the *abgrund*, the unground, there is neither politics nor ethics. Schelling evokes this problem as essentially a question of evil: evil arises when an active selfhood that seeks its actualization, seeks to appropriate its own condition so that there be no more scission of ground and existence, in other words, man in evil—since only man can be evil—seeks to appropriate what is non-appropriable, what it should have kept as *mere ground*, what it should not have sought to arouse into active self-hood. The task of the political is to open itself to the non-appropriability of *abgrund*, in other words, to carry the traces of the finitude that marks the opening, that opens to *polis*, which also means, to carry the traces of the scission, the rupture, the interruption that opens so that there be infinite opening, always to come.

There seems already a problematic here, an aporia of the political: for is it not that the very non-appropriability of the opening itself calls forth all the works of appropriation so that the non-appropriation no longer remains non-appropriation, or rather, is it not the unnamable and undecidable itself that calls forth all that names and over names and all that must be decided, so that the undecidable no longer remains undecidable and the unnamable no longer remains unnamable, in other words, that which would make evil itself possible, for what is evil if not the appropriating of the non-appropriable, naming what is not nameable, deciding what should have remained in excess of any judgment of decision? Is it not in the opening where there also occurs the opening of evil, of the very possibility of evil: is not the evil that arises into active selfhood in this opening, as the very possibility of the mark, the very possibility of the scission, the interruption, the very name in which evil speaks? To bring in Schelling again, should not God, in revealing, also reveal the very possibility of evil, for the revelation marks the very possibility of a scission of ground and existence, the interruption and rupture of the non-appropriability and appropriation, in the very possibility of finitude? Would not then a melancholy, a more primordial melancholy than man, have darkened God's being too, for in revealing existence, in separating ground and existence, God would also have seen the very possibility of a darkening of existence, the very possibility of evil? Should God then not have revealed himself, and not revealed himself in nature and to man? That would have been absurd, Schelling answers, for evil does not lie in finitude in-itself, nor in revelation-in-itself, but finite's being's, in his/her desire for actualization, seeking to appropriate what ought to remain as *mere ground*, to keep evil as a *mere possibility*; instead, there is revelation so that love pervades, which is distorted in evil, and there occurs a perverse inversion of the principles. There is evil neither in the very opening of the polis, nor in the interruption that marks the opening, though evil speaks in its name, in the name of an interruption, for evil—if we follow Schelling—does not have its own name, it is not being; evil lies not in naming itself as such, however, but in—I will speak of Benjamin here—in overnaming, in seeking to exhaust the unnamable in overnaming, in seeking to appropriate the unnameable and reducing it to significations. Evil of the politics does not lie in finitude of the opening itself as such—for there is evil, far more frightening and terrible evil when there is no opening at all—but evil rather lies in seeking to appropriate this very opening, to exhaust it in the works of significations, to reduce it to the works of negativity and death, for this work of death does not know the other death, death that is not negative, death whose mourning is inconsolable. Rather the system of signification annuls the other death, by seeking to exhaust the other's death in significations, in seeking to overname the mourning that marks the very finitude of the other, for can there be *polis* without this finitude, without the works of simultaneous exclusion and inclusion, expulsion and appropriation, in having to name the unnamable that suspends the very name? Does not the opening, thus, mark the violence of the rupture, thus the very possibility and *force* of the law, the law-instituting *force*, the violence that exiles the one who names the unnamable, and in naming, also opens the possibility of *polis*, of politics as such, and hence the possibility of law, its *force* and its judgment? Is not any possibility of *polis* also a matter of absolute decision—or it is already decided by undecidable so that it is decidable—and that this decision, deciding *at the limit*, as an experience of impossibility, institutes the *force* that must accompany every decision, the violence of decision, the *force* of appropriating and naming the non-appropriable and the nameless?

What of the name, then? What of the violence of language? What of the gift? Can there be gift without naming the unnamable, without the name, without *force* in having to name the other, violence to the other, in which case there will not be a gift? Can there be a gift at all? Or rather, can there be a gift at all without a certain melancholy that marks in all gifts, in all giving and offering, that inhibits in the very giving, even if it is giving the name, even if the name-giver be the God-like, that names what is pure naming? In *Trauerspiel* book, Benjamin says,

> To be named—even if the name-giver is god-like and saintly—perhaps always brings with it a presentiment of mourning. But how much so not to be named, only to be read, uncertainly by the allegorist, and to have become highly significant only to him. (Benjamin 1998: 224–5)

Again in another place,

> To be named—even when the name is godlike and blissful—perhaps always remains an intimation of mourning. But how much

> more melancholy it is to be named not from the one blessed paradisiacal language of names, but from the hundred languages of man, in which name has already withered, yet which, according to God's pronouncement, have knowledge of things. (Benjamin 1996: 73)

That means melancholy, an intimation of mournfulness already *affects* the very possibility of naming, in having to name what does not yet have a name, what is nameless and mute. Having to name what is yet to have a name, what is to come, what is to be named, the naming of the poets *endow* what is named with mournfulness. This mournfulness affects the opening, or rather the *poesis* of the opening already opens itself to mournfulness, or would we say, opening itself is this mournfulness, because already in the opening, there opens the lament of the nameless in being endowed with the name. Is this not that which affects the poets and philosophers—the name-givers—and therefore they are, amongst all, the most mournful? It is not, however, only that the nameless mourns in being endowed with the name, but that there is also a mournfulness that makes nature mute. Benjamin brings the proposition to the sharpest point of paradox: not only the mournfulness that makes nature mute, but also the inverse proposition is true as well: she is mute and therefore she mourns,

> It is a metaphysical truth that all nature would begin to lament if it were endowed with language... This proposition has a double meaning. It means, first, that she would lament language itself. Speechlessness: that is the great sorrow of nature (and for the sake of her redemption the life and language of *man*—not only, as is supposed, of the poet—are in nature). This proposition means, second, that she would lament. Lament, however, is the most undifferentiated, impotent expression of language. It contains scarcely more than the sensuous breath; and even where there is only a rustling of plants, there is always a lament. Because she is mute, nature mourns. Yet the inverse proposition leads even further into the essence of nature; the sadness of nature makes her mute. (Benjamin 1996: 73)

There is, however, other mourning—otherwise than the mourning of the mute, the mute lament and otherwise even than the mourning in being named, the name that redeems the speechlessness of the nameless; the other mourning is in being *overnamed*, when the name itself withers away, when the name becomes a mere *means*. The *overnaming* reduces the naming into significance, when the immediacy of the communication is lost in the mediacy of the significance and there arises the mythic violence of the law:

> There is, in the relation of human languages to that of things, something that can be approximately described as "overnaming"—the deepest linguistic reason for all melancholy and (from the point of view of thing) for all deliberate muteness. (Benjamin 1996: 73)

Benjamin speaks of it as fall: the loss of the name in the language of judgment, in signification in which the names occurs as mere instruments, as mere means, as mere medium; in other words, language becomes mediated in the language of judgment, and the name is hollowed inside out, becomes hollow and empty in the bubbling and prattling. Here also takes the mythic birth of law and *force* of it: the nameless is sought to be appropriated in overnaming that now assumes the language of judgment and significance, in the name of law and its *force*. The magic of the prattle is the very magic of evil, which has to be differentiated from the magic of the name. Before in the name, the name communicates nothing but that which communicates itself in the name; but now name becomes mere means, and the name falls outside itself, it is made to signify what comes from outside of itself, namely, knowledge of good and evil, for 'evil abandons the name' (Benjamin 1996: 71). What evil abandons, in the mere instrumentalzation of the name, not only the name, but abandons the very gift of language, gift that is given to man independently of him.

Schelling calls the gift a "loan". Thus Schelling finds the melancholy of nature and all finite beings in this experience of evil. Man's language and man's condition is gift, a "loan" given to him independently, so that in the non-appropriability of his condition, in the non-conditionality of the gift man opens himself to the opening of his active self-hood, so that there be the *polis*, which is nothing but opening towards *the being-towards-others*, so that in naming the lament of the nameless being carries over as responsibility to the nameless or for what is yet to be named. In Schelling's words, that there be love and that there be infinite freedom of creating and revealing[2]. Therefore the gift, the *loan* itself is the very conditionality of the *Polis*, of the political, of love, of freedom and that itself for that matter, which is the gift of finitude—finitude because the ground eludes all acts of grounding, and hence *abgrund*, the unground—is not evil in itself. The evil lies in the ingratitude towards the gift, in denying responsibility for the inheriting of the debt, of the "loan", in seeking to appropriate the gift in the overnaming and in the judgment, in the valiant assertion of the mythic origin of the law, without seeing that it has its conditionality somewhere else, in the gift itself, in the gift of the name. There is a nobility and dignity of the name, even though it is too affected by mourning. Benjamin evokes Friedrich Müller here: 'Friedrich Müller has Adam say of the animals that leave him after he has named them, 'And saw by the nobility with which they leaped away from me that the man had given them a name" (Benjamin 1996: 72). But with overnaming, Benjamin says, there begins the other lament, the other mourning, lament that laments the forgetting of the gift and loss of the dignity of the name. In the opening of *polis* too, the opening is affected by mourning, for opening always opens in the name, in the naming and for which this mournfulness affects the one who names—the poets and philosophers—and there is mourning, for opening in the naming is already marked by the interruption of non-appropriability and appropriation, of the nameless and the name, of non-conditional condition and conditioned, the *abgrund* of the ground and grounding: the political is the very task that keeps open to this interruption, to this scission of this opening. But since non-appropriability also calls forth appropriation, the nameless, the name and *abgrund* all works of grounding, there also occurs the other mourning at the very closure of the interruption, the very reification and annihilation of the name into the abyss of signification where name is a mere means. This means mourning marks the limit of all works of significations, mourning that mourns at the limit of what constitutes a certain closure of politics, closure that seeks to close the very possibility of opening and seeks to appropriate the non-appropriable, in other words, it forgets the finitude that opens the political and *polis*. If mourning carries incessantly the gift of finitude, the very gift of naming, from the immemorial times, it also thereby, at the very limit of the *polis*, keeps open to the gift, gift of the event, gift of the coming of the other. Gift always comes as surprise: gift that is already known, calculated in advance, and known by the knowable is not a gift. If the gift of language is inseparable from mourning, it is because one who mourns, in the words of Benjamin, 'feels itself thoroughly known by the unknowable' (Benjamin 1996: 73). This gift, the gift of the name, inseparable from an experience of finitude and mourning, is also thereby an experience of renouncing of *force,* of law-positing violence: to think of the gift without "force" of judgment and law-positing force, would be to think that which renounces force by interrupting forces. *Gift renounces force by interrupting forces*: mourning or death is this very interruption. Thus Derrida says: 'Death, or rather mourning, the mourning of the absolute of force: that is the name, or one of the names, of this affect that unites force to the without force, thereby relating the manifestation of force, as image, to the being without force of *that which* it manifests or lets be seen, right before our eyes and according to our mourning' (Derrida 1996: 177). If there is "force" of gift, and for that matter "force" of mourning, it lies in the renunciation of forces, as interruption of forces: this renunciation of forces that constitutes or deconstitutes "force" of mourning, mourning of the gift, affects the very moment of decision, gives decision its "force". Therefore decisions are always taken at the limit, which means, decisions are always a certain experience of death and mourning, a certain impossibility and endurance. There lies the sadness of the gift of the name, the lament in naming: it lies in renunciation of forces, of possessions; it marks the very limit of *polis*, or the limit of the theologico-political foundation of community, it marks the limit of language itself. Thus Heidegger says of the gift,

> … Real renouncement, in other words one which carries itself authentically, is a power of creation and engendering. By letting go of its old possessions it receives a gift, but not after the fact,

> as a reward: for within it the mournful endurance of necessary renouncement and giving away is a "receiving". (Heidegger 1980: 94)

In another place Heidegger thinks the gift of the naming as call, calling to arrive, a call to come, welcoming itself, for which we must be *thankful* for the gift: 'All naming and all being named is the familiar 'to call' only because naming itself consists by nature in the real calling, in the call to come, in a commending and a command' (Heidegger 1968: 120). And further,

> To call is not originally to name, but the other way around: naming is a kind of calling, in the original sense of demanding and commending. It is not that the call has its being in the name; rather every name is a kind of call. Every call implies an approach. We might call a guest welcome. (Heidegger 1968: 125)

Is not what we have been attempting to think of the event, the event of coming, that in naming the name calls, welcomes, is always the gift: the gift of the name that calls, calls for the event to come; it welcomes in hospitality for the event to arrive? Without this hospitality of the name and its call, there is neither politics nor ethics; without this gift of the name, "no thing may be":

> So I renounced and sadly see:
> Where word breaks off no thing may be.

Notes

1. Thus Heidegger says, 'The opening would not be mere opening of presence, but the opening of presence concealing itself, the opening of a self-concealing sheltering' (1978, p. 391).
2. Thus Schelling says: 'But the question why God did not prefer not to reveal himself at all, since he necessarily foresaw the evil would at least follow as an accompaniment of Self-revelation, this question really deserves no reply. For this would be as much as saying that love itself should not be, so that there could be no contrast to love; that is, the absolutely positive should be sacrificed to the merely temporal. We have already explained that God's self-revelation should be regarded not as an unconditioned, arbitrary act, but as an act morally necessary, in which love and goodness triumphed over absolute inwardness. Thus if God had not revealed himself on account of evil, evil would have been victorious over

goodness and love' (82–83). And again: 'The will of the depths must abide its freedom till all has been fulfilled, till all has become real. If it were conquered sooner, the good would remain concealed in it together with evil. But the good is to be raised out of darkness to actuality in order to dwell with God everlastingly; and the evil is to be separated from goodness in order to be cast out eternally into non-being. For this is the final purpose of creation, that that which could not be in itself, shall be in itself through being raised out of darkness as a depth independent of God, and elevated into existence. Hence the necessity of birth and death...thus in its freedom the basis effects the separation and judgment and in this very way accomplishes God's complete actualization' (Schelling 1936: 84–85).

References

Aristotle, 'Problems Connected with Prudence, Intelligence and Wisdom', in Book XXX, *The Works of Aristotle, Vol. VII, Problemata,* trans, E.S. Forster (Oxford: Clarendon Press, 1971).

Benjamin, Walter, *The Origin of German Tragic Drama,* trans. John Osborne (London and New York: Verso, 1998).

Benjamin, Walter, 'On Language as Such and the Language of Man' in *Selected Writings,* Vol. 1: 1913-1926, eds. Marcus Bullock and Michael W. Jennings(Cambridge & Massachusetts: The Belknap Press of Harvard University Press, 1996).

Derrida, Jacques, 'By Force of Mourning' in *Critical Inquiry,* Vol. 22, no. 2 (1996), 171–192.

Derrida, Jacques, *Specters of Marx: The State of the Debt, the Work of Mourning and the New International,* trans. Peggy Kamuf (London and New York: Routledge, 1994).

Heidegger, Martin, *Introduction to Metaphysics,* trans. Ralph Manheim (Delhi: Motilal Benarassidass, 1999).

Heidegger, Martin, 'The End of Philosophy and the Task of Thinking' in *Basic Writings,* ed. David Farrell, Krell (London & Henley: Routledge and Kegan Paul, 1978).

Heidegger, Martin, 'Hölderlins Hymnen "Germanien" and "Der Rhein"' in *Gesamtausgabe,* Vol. 39 (Frankfurt am Main: Vitoria Klostermann, 1980).

Heidegger, Martin, *What is Called Thinking,* Fred D. Wieck and J. Glenn Gray (New York & Evanston: Harper and Row, 1968).

Schelling, F.W.J., *Philosophical Inquiries into the Nature of Human Freedom,* trans. James Gutmann (La Salle, Illinois: Open Court, 1936).

Contributors

Swarnika Ahuja is a painter and academician. She is completing her Masters from Centre for English Studies, Jawaharlal Nehru University.

Sneha Chowdhury is currently pursuing her M.Phil research on Paul Celan at the Centre for English Studies, Jawaharlal Nehru University. She is interested in aesthetic theories and phenomenology.

Priyanka Das is pursuing her doctoral degree from the Centre for English Studies, Jawaharlal Nehru University. She has worked on objectification of male body for her M.Phil. Currently she is working on the politics of Visuality in "Game of Thrones".

Saitya Brata Das teaches philosophy and literature at the Centre for English Studies, Jawaharlal Nehru University. He is the author of *The Political Theology of Schelling* (Edinburgh University Press, 2016).

Soumick De has worked on the concept of theatre in the Christian Middle Ages for his PhD from the School of Arts and Aesthetics, Jawaharlal Nehru University. His areas of interest include: contemporary French thought and Christian theology of the Middle Ages.

Anup Dhar teaches at the School of Human Studies, and Director, Ambedkar University, Delhi, India. His areas of interest include: Marxism, Developmental Economics, Psychoanalysis, Gender and Sexuality Studies.

Huzaifa Omair Siddiqi is a PhD Research Scholar and UGC-Junior Research Fellow at the Centre for English Studies, Jawaharlal Nehru University. His current research revolves around Michel Henry's phenomenological concept of life.

Krishnan Unni is a novelist and academician. He teaches literature at Deshbandhu College of Delhi University. He works on contemporary critical theory and contemporary French thought.